Early Praise for *Courageous Clarity*

"For accomplished leaders looking for a jump start and rising leaders thinking about what's next, the tools and insights in *Courageous Clarity* will challenge you to think differently about how to move forward in your leadership journey."
—**Julie Woolf, COO, The Argen Corporation**

"Phyllis Sarkaria's work with executives and leaders at all levels brings rich insight and depth to the tools that she describes in *Courageous Clarity*. This book is a must read for any leader who wants to gain clarity and step boldly toward their professional goals."
—**Douglas C. Bryant, President & CEO, Quidel Corporation**

"*Courageous Clarity* puts tools immediately in the hands of organizations that lack time and resources to develop their leaders. The accessible and relevant examples and exercises pave the way for supporting the new world of work."
—**Desiree Therianos, VP, People, Okera**

"In this book, Phyllis Sarkaria presents actionable tools, razor-sharp insights, and real-life stories for leaders seeking to create more respectful, inclusive teams by exercising curiosity, building trust, and increasing awareness of how their work impacts others."
—**CB Bowman, MCEC, CMC, BCC, CEO, Association of Corporate Executive Coaches and CEO, Workplace Equity & Equality**

"*Courageous Clarity* contains information that is useful for a wide range of leaders, those early in their career journeys and those with more experience. Each will take away something unique and personalized that will benefit their leadership development."
—**Randall Clark, SVP and CHRO, Sempra Infrastructure**

"This book has many insightful anecdotes that drive home the points in ways that are both entertaining and educational. I recommend it for anyone who is looking for an opportunity to advance their career in a meaningful way. Having worked with Phyllis Sarkaria for over a year, I know that she speaks with authority in her support of leadership growth."
—**Stephen J. Conroy, PhD, Professor of Economics, University of San Diego School of Business**

"*Courageous Clarity* is full of valuable examples and recommendations for taking a thoughtful approach to leadership. The many tools will help you make change in the right direction."
—**Devyani Bedekar, Director, Global Product Management, ConvaTec**

"You may have ideas about how you would like your career to evolve. Figuring out the best path to get where you want to be can be a challenge, even for successful leaders. *Courageous Clarity* helps you map a leadership journey to achieve your dreams."
—**Johannes Kehle, R&D Executive & Managing Director, Quidel Germany GmbH**

"With its accessible style, resonant case studies, and reflective questions, *Courageous Clarity* is a must-pack item for those looking to make the most of their leadership journey."
—**Samantha L. Forusz, former HR leader, Performance and Development, The World Bank Group**

"Through stories and exercises, Phyllis Sarkaria provides successful leaders with knowledge and skills to manage 'the wild ride' of leadership in today's culturally diverse, volatile and complex world."
—**Jordan Goldrich, MCEC, PCC, and Amazon best-selling co-author of *Workplace Warrior, People Skills for the No-Bullshit Executive***

"*Courageous Clarity* is an indispensable roadmap for those new to, or preparing for, senior leadership positions who want to best meet the challenges of higher-level leadership."
—**Jack Farnan, VP, Human Resources, HM Electronics**

Courageous Clarity

Courageous

Clarity

NAVIGATING
THE WAY FORWARD
ON YOUR LEADERSHIP
JOURNEY

Phyllis H. Sarkaria

Copyright © 2022 Phyllis H. Sarkaria.
All rights reserved.

Although the information in this book has great value, there are no guarantees regarding its usefulness. Kind of like life. If you insist on a guarantee, leadership may not be for you. Neither the author nor the publisher shall be liable or responsible for any loss or damage resulting from the reader's use, application, implementation, or imitation of any information or ideas presented in this book. The discussion of activities, approaches, and exercises in this book is not intended as a substitute for consulting with a qualified professional coach or adviser to obtain advice and support relevant to the individual's situation. Each reader must assume responsibility for his or her own actions. In short, this book and its contents are provided as-is with no warranty of any kind.

The examples and case studies in this book are based on information from client engagements and interviews with C-suite leaders. While this is a work of non-fiction, names and identifying details have been combined, changed, and omitted to protect client privacy.

Paperback ISBN: 979-8-9852707-0-9
Hardback ISBN: 979-8-9852707-1-6
Ebook ISBN: 979-8-9852707-2-3

Library of Congress Control Number: 2021925297

Published by
The Sarkaria Group LLC
P.O. Box 22159
San Diego, CA 92192

For Max, Maddie, Mia, Morgan, and Evie:

May you have the courage to remain curious about yourself and the people around you throughout your life. When you do, amazing discoveries are possible.

Contents

Preface xiii

Introduction 1

Chapter 1—A Spirit of Discovery 15

Chapter 2—Ask the Locals 37

Chapter 3—Trust as a Bridge to Success 55

Chapter 4—Finding the Path Forward 73

Chapter 5—Managing the Inevitable Detour 93

Chapter 6—When the Obstacle *Is* the Opportunity 111

Chapter 7—It's Not All Smooth Sailing 133

Final Thoughts 157

Endnotes 163

Acknowledgments 171

Index 175

About the Author 183

Preface

It's the rare person who knows exactly what they want to do in life and doggedly follows that path. Most of us find ourselves on a journey with many twists and turns. For some, the road is smooth and the view is great. For others, there are often detours and unexpected changes in the itinerary. I've learned that those bumps in the road can lead to some pretty interesting outcomes when you remain curious and persistent.

In college, I considered a few different paths, eventually embarking on one, thanks to encouragement from well-meaning family members, but my diverse interests and innate curiosity took me in another direction. First, I sought an MBA to remedy the crushing boredom induced by my first career choice. I eventually spent ten years as an energy industry lobbyist, working with customers, identifying opportunities for collaboration, and engaging in strategic planning and negotiation. Those experiences included a detour for a couple of years with a boutique consulting firm, where I developed my research, writing, and public speaking chops. Simultaneously, I began teaching in the evenings and discovered what would become an enduring love of mentoring and supporting the development of others.

Those early career moves were marked by some consistent threads. First, I found myself returning to questions that intrigued me regarding the sociology of business. Why do people behave the way they do in companies? What motivates them? I was fascinated by human dynamics and how those resulted in the success—or failure—of people and organizations. Second, at my core, I've always been something of a nerd. I played chess in high school and learned a fundamental skill: how to scan the board several moves ahead to anticipate my opponent's moves and see where I needed to go. It turns out this forward-looking approach is an ideal lens to puzzle through why people behave in certain ways. It has helped me address issues before they arise and is a perspective that continues to serve me well.

The many zigzags in my path steered me toward an opportunity to spend a few years in human resources before taking an operational role. Little did I know at the time that HR would be my dream job and I would never make it to Operations. Human resources brought together the myriad skills and interests I had pursued for years. I subsequently served almost two decades in senior HR leadership roles, where I honed my influence and team-building skills and spent countless hours coaching executives and high-potential leaders. I also continued to teach at the university level, guiding and encouraging working adults who were ready for new career directions. In all this work, I found my passion. The opportunity to increase success through good people practices was addictive—and I was hooked!

The coaching aspect of my work as a corporate leader was not only the most personally fulfilling, it was where I felt

PREFACE

I could make the most impact. For the executives I supported, I was their thought partner, collaborative problem-solver, and sounding board. They expected me to hold them accountable and discuss tough issues with them. This work brought immense satisfaction and allowed me to truly have a positive impact.

While fulfilling, my professional path has not always been sunshine and roses. Like most people, I've run into difficult circumstances and problematic colleagues, but every challenge was a chance to learn. If I'm honest, the most frustrating situations and difficult individuals taught me something about myself. Considering how best to counter opposition to a proposal raised my level of performance as I thought about ways to improve my ideas. Running into roadblocks caused me to pause and consider alternative paths. Ultimately the organizations and the people I served benefited from the extra effort that those encounters required of me. I was unwilling to rest on my past success and took risks to grow. Eventually this required making the very difficult decision to leave a job and team that I had loved when I realized I was no longer enthusiastic about the road ahead and needed to make a change.

Every obstacle I encountered in my career was an opportunity for reflection and improvement. That continues to be true today. By 2016, finding less inspiration in my day-to-day responsibilities, I decided to take the leap from in-house-corporate roles. After considering a few options, I decided to build a practice that would enable me to work with a broader and more diverse group of leaders. Certification from the

Berkeley Executive Coaching Institute and an additional graduate degree—this one in ethical leadership—from Claremont Lincoln University, coupled with my professional experience, provided further credentials as I established myself as a management consultant and leadership coach.

The methodology I use for coaching—the foundation for the approach outlined in this book—evolved from these educational opportunities and my decades in the corporate trenches, as well as my leadership consulting and teaching. And while I'm always learning and adapting my approach, now seemed like a good time to share the process that has helped so many people achieve breakthroughs in their leadership. Sometimes clients have remarked that the solutions they have discovered seem simplistic, even obvious, but it wasn't until they uncovered what was getting in their way that they could continue on a path to success. That's the magic of this work.

Our world has become increasingly complex and uncertain. Now, more than ever, organizations need leaders who are empathetic, humble, and eager to learn, serve, and share their expertise. Such leaders are better equipped to engage and guide teams in spite of ambiguity and volatility. My coaching practice is focused on helping leaders enhance their self-awareness and develop skills to create greater impact in their roles. The approach I outline here is far from radical. In fact, it's quite simple. But as most of us know, simple doesn't always translate to easy. It takes intention and practice. Whether you're an emerging leader looking for a leg up or a seasoned executive in need of new ideas or a reset, my

PREFACE

hope is that you'll find inspiration through the stories and techniques in these pages.

The truth is, I've learned more from my colleagues and clients than I suspect they've ever gotten from me. For that, I owe all of them a huge debt of gratitude. Here's to continuing the journey together and finding opportunity in each and every jog in the road.

Introduction

"Leadership is a process of social influence, which maximizes the efforts of others, towards achievement of a goal."

— KEVIN KRUSE, CEO OF LEADx

Leadership is not for the faint of heart. It can be a wild ride—fun, scary, and exhilarating—sometimes all at once. At its best, leading others is an incredibly fulfilling experience. You delight in the shared thrill of achieving things as a team that you didn't think possible. You tap depths and talents in yourself you didn't know you possessed. On the flipside, leadership can feel like bumping up against one obstacle after another, arriving at dead ends that leave you depleted and discouraged. Most leaders experience both edges of the spectrum, often multiple times in their leadership journey. It takes **courage** to be a leader. And to be a good leader, or daresay a great one, it takes **clarity**. *Courageous Clarity* combines stories of leaders who have done the hard work to become truly good leaders, along with proven techniques for gaining the clarity that is essential to effective leadership.

Over the years, successful leaders have applied solid management practices—much like the information contained in these pages—to thrive in their roles. They were driven to achieve, took on additional responsibilities, and applied their talents. When they stumbled along the way, those leaders realized they had been relying on old maps for the leadership journey ahead. They are not alone. A number of sources, including The Corporate Executive Board and Heidrick & Struggles, have estimated that at least half of all new executives falter or fail within the first eighteen months, and more than that fail to live up to the expectations of those who appoint them. Fortunately, the tools contained in this book are available to help you stay on track and find your way back if you get off course. These tools highlight the importance of soft skills as a measure of success—curiosity, trust, humility, communication—versus title and salary alone.

If you are not willing to settle for where you are, exercising *courageous clarity* may be for you. Are you committed to continuous growth and improvement to build on past achievements? Curiosity, balanced with ambition, can help you let go of old habits and rethink what will make you successful. Are you willing to take on broader responsibilities in an effort to grow and thrive? When you're open to new ideas, you will be able to overcome the inevitable setbacks and disappointments you encounter along the path of your leadership journey.

Maybe you are a seasoned corporate leader dealing with new challenges. Perhaps you joined a new company in the last year or two, recently got a new boss, or you are seeking your first executive position. You might have had one (or more) of these conversations with yourself:

- Success has always been easy. All of a sudden, it isn't. I want to be seen as an expert and a trusted colleague. How do I move forward and deal productively with detours and distractions?

- I've always been highly regarded in this organization, but I'm not sure our new CEO sees my value. How do I validate my contribution and get back on track?

INTRODUCTION

- I know I'm talented or they wouldn't have hired me. I really need to deliver on these goals, but what I've done before just isn't working in this situation. What now?

- Should I have taken this job? What was I thinking? These people don't appreciate me. Have I derailed my career with this move?

Leadership is a journey. It is not a linear path, nor a destination. Knowing where you are at any point along the way is important, just as it is vital to know where you want to go. Sometimes it is necessary to pause, refuel, or reconsider where you are headed. Good leadership is not achieved through a set formula (i.e., do these four things and you will be wildly successful). If only it were that straightforward. Like any journey, there are commonalities that contribute to a positive experience for anyone, but what makes for a great trip is unique to each person. Leadership is no different. *Courageous Clarity* can help you find your way as a leader.

A little navigational support is useful in any journey. That's certainly true for the leadership journey. It used to be that having a decent map was sufficient to stay on course. With the advent of GPS, however, we've grown accustomed to having a ready guide that tells us where we are at the moment, provides options for the path forward, and helps us make adjustments and respond to unforeseen changes. For me, GPS has another meaning. It has been a game-changer in terms of how I think about navigating challenges in the professional world. As I've worked with corporate leaders, it has become a natural way for me to think about the dynamic nature of leadership.

GPS provides a structure to guide your path on the leadership journey. The ideas and exercises you are about to discover have been road tested. They work and will help you get on track and stay the course. The tips and techniques that will make the most positive difference for you depend on your style, your organization's culture, and the people on your team.

Get ready for the journey. A packing list ensures you have what you need. This is about increasing self-awareness, the inner journey, and your preparation.

Pay attention along the way. Watch for sign posts to stay on track. You might need to make adjustments to your inner leadership journey or adapt how you relate to others in order to reach your goals. As you come to know yourself better, adding tools to engage and inspire others will benefit your success as a leader.

Slow down to assess and adjust. It may be wise to exercise caution at some point on your journey. It is a fortunate traveler who doesn't need to occasionally pause and reassess. Whether you've inadvertently created your own problems, or people and events outside of your control have impacted your progress, the savvy traveler is prepared for the unexpected.

INTRODUCTION

Think in terms of preparation and agility for both anticipated curves and unexpected bumps in the road. This mindset acknowledges that there are some elements of any journey over which you have complete control; others you can effectively manage, though they will always be out of your direct control. Many aspects of the leadership journey require partnership with other leaders and with team members. The ability to develop positive working relationships is a common attribute of effective leaders. It is increasingly important as you rise in an organization. Getting relationships right is aided by GPS.

HOW TO GET THE MOST OUT OF THIS BOOK

Whatever your challenge or frustration in your current role, you are not alone. Others have made this journey, overcoming issues to successfully reach their destination. The stories I share in *Courageous Clarity* are drawn from my experiences with colleagues and clients. While I've changed some details to protect confidentiality, the situations are representative of common leadership challenges. You might even recognize yourself or people you know in these stories. My hope is that the scenarios help you better understand how to put these concepts into practice. Each section of the book includes exercises for those who would like to take action. There are also questions for reflection at the end of each chapter.

The ideas, exercises, tips, and tools in this book are effective—they work. Any individual can achieve change through dedicated practice. You may want to find a trusted friend or colleague who will serve as an accountability partner. To accelerate your progress, you might consider engaging a leadership coach to help you make sustainable change toward your goals.

Experiment with how best to engage with the material. Some readers find it useful to skim the book first, then return to chapters that are most relevant to the challenges they're currently facing. Others prefer to tackle the book chapter by chapter, sticking with the concepts until they are mastered. There's no one right way to benefit from *Courageous Clarity*. The important thing is to be persistent and patient with yourself and others. With practice, you can achieve results with these tools.

Beyond the references to research in the body of the book, I've included additional resources in the endnotes, should you be interested in exploring some of the concepts in greater detail. There are many outstanding researchers and practitioners working in the fields of leadership and management. I encourage you to delve into their work to learn more.

AN IMPORTANT NOTE ON CULTURAL DIFFERENCES

Courageous Clarity is written from a US-centric point of view. In our world today, most organizations have some level of international presence, even if they are not truly multinational. Communication nuances, comfort in speaking up to share information with those in power, and perceptions of organizational politics differ widely across cultures.

Here is a simple example with several points that make our interconnectedness real. Rebecca is a senior executive who took

INTRODUCTION

a position with a German company owned by a British firm. Rebecca is American. Though she spoke the same language as the corporate owners, colloquialisms and slang were different. This created communication missteps, raised frustrations, and impacted trust.

Further, within the organization she led, Rebecca soon learned that delegating would not be easy. She had to teach her German team members that it was okay to take action without her. This was counter to their professional understanding and German culture. They believed the boss should make all the decisions. For example, Rebecca found that, while she was on vacation, people delayed action until she was back in the office. From her holiday, she sent messages encouraging them to move forward. Some warmly embraced the opportunity to run with their solutions. Others weren't comfortable and waited until she returned. Rebecca wanted her team to trust that she meant it when she said she would delegate certain decisions. If they got it wrong, they got it wrong and everyone learned. It took time and patience for Rebecca to understand the cultural influences that caused them to hold back. Her team also needed time, and experience under Rebecca's leadership, to trust they could behave differently and succeed.

Communication nuances, comfort in speaking up to those in power, and perceptions of organizational politics differ widely across cultures.

This is an elementary example of cultural awareness in an environment that might seem fairly homogeneous. At the same time, the story highlights the complexities of people from different cultures working together. You may be leading employees who show more (or less) deference to power, are not comfortable speaking up even when invited, or who prize saving face above all else. Openness, curiosity, and flexibility—key attributes discussed in this book—can help those who are not accustomed to interacting with different cultures. Appreciating diversity of thought and the influence of each person's culture on their behavior can go a long way toward working well together.

Stay curious, listen, and take responsibility to establish trust. The clarity arising from these actions will open the door to greater adventures on your continuing leadership journey.

PREVIEW OF THE JOURNEY

Here's what you can expect on a chapter-by-chapter basis and an introduction to the people you'll meet along the way.

Chapter 1 – A Spirit of Discovery. Every journey requires a certain amount of preparation. Even if this is not your first leadership journey, each role you hold represents a new path. Just as a mountain climber doesn't stop training once they crest their first peak, leaders must recognize the need for continued growth to build on past successes. It is the leadership equivalent of staying in shape along the way. This journey begins with insights into how leadership benefits from

INTRODUCTION

curiosity, humility, and reflection, and provides exercises to strengthen those practices.

> **MEET SAM:** newly appointed VP of a rapidly growing startup and responsible for mergers and acquisitions. In his eagerness to get a quick win and help a senior colleague out of a jam, Sam ends up with a mess on his hands.

Chapter 2 – Ask the Locals. As competent as you are, there are still things you will miss when you believe in yourself too strongly. Understand the power of muting yourself to turn up listening and seek new viewpoints, the key to gaining information you need in your role. A fresh perspective can be realized by asking others to provide you with future-focused feedback or "feedforward." Stop talking. Really listen to what they have to say.

> **MEET AMARA:** second-in-command of a large business unit of an established corporation. While known for her excellent results, Amara is not tuned in to her team. Her tendency to hold tightly to her limited perspective and ignore potential blind spots is getting the better of her.

Chapter 3 – Trust as a Bridge to Success. Trust is foundational for any team to function well. As you come to know yourself and your team members better, how can you bring out others' best—their superpowers—to create an environment where your team is capable of going the distance? This chapter explores how to more quickly establish trusting work relationships, diagnose when trust is not forthcoming, and transparently interact to strengthen connections with colleagues.

> MEET CLARE AND MARK: New to her role as an R&D executive with a fast-growing biotech company, Clare's colleagues were thrilled to have her join the team because of her depth of expertise. But the excitement wears off as trust issues emerge and upend the team dynamics. On the flip side is Mark, whose secret weapon is the "bank of trust" that leads to team loyalty and strong results.

Chapter 4 – Finding the Path Forward. Take a look at your actions as a leader. In this chapter, you will explore a different way of thinking about leadership presence and how to bring that presence to your interactions. Doing so will help you process information and separate facts from assumptions. The result: you'll manage your reactions better, thoughtfully respond, and seek a solid path forward.

> MEET MARCUS: an Operations executive with a multinational corporation. He learns the importance of getting beyond his own baggage and assumptions when he confronts the CFO about perceived missteps.

Chapter 5 – Managing the Inevitable Detour. On any journey, detours may be unavoidable. You are under tremendous pressure to deliver results. Refining your powers of observation can help you anticipate and bypass obstacles in your path,

INTRODUCTION

but don't try to handle these challenges alone. Remaining open to collaboration can bring greater focus and insight to the actions you need to take. This flexibility will also help you identify priorities, determine how to move forward, and address challenges with agility and tact.

> **MEET ALINA, RANDALL, AND VICTOR:** a newly appointed COO for a large regional bank, a tech sales company executive, and a community organizer, respectively. Each is facing challenges that come from getting distracted and losing focus on the things that really matter.

Chapter 6 – When the Obstacle Is the Opportunity. Building on the idea that every leadership journey experiences detours and challenges at some point, this chapter identifies communication tools intended to help you overcome obstacles. There is a specific focus on influence and constructive conflict-resolution skills with a goal of productively managing conflict and influencing better outcomes. Familiarity with, or reintroduction of, these tools in your daily work can help you collaborate in environments, old and new, to achieve amazing results.

> **MEET CARLA:** the blunt, direct new boss of a team of manufacturing leaders. Her "tell-sell-yell" approach to management is undercutting performance.

Chapter 7 – It's Not All Smooth Sailing. After looking at the positive side of leadership and many "right" things that you can do as a leader, it is important to acknowledge that challenges exist in any organization. Not everything is under your control—and even if it is, there are limits. Sometimes things just don't work out. To make a strong, meaningful impact, you can't underestimate the importance of understanding how to positively navigate around turbulence and minefields. Even in the best organizations, there will occasionally be rough patches. How you respond to these situations is evidence of your leadership.

MEET JOHN, ANDY, BARBARA, SCOTT, SANTIAGO, AND ED: six leaders with diverse positions and personalities. They navigate the challenges of organizational politics with varying degrees of skill—and very different outcomes.

TRAVEL JOURNAL

At the end of each chapter, you will be invited to reflect on what you have read. Keep these broader issues in mind when addressing the specific questions of each chapter.

- How does the information apply to your current leadership situation?
- What would you like to change?
- How can you use what you learned from the chapter?

INTRODUCTION

In each instance, you may want to record notes that you can reference later. Just as travelers often jot down a few thoughts while on an extended vacation, think of these notes—in whatever form you capture them—as a travel journal for your leadership journey.

CHAPTER 1

A Spirit of Discovery

"The best in business have boundless curiosity and open minds."
— ROBIN SHARMA, LEADERSHIP EXPERT

Consider your most recent trip. Maybe it was a quick weekend getaway. Perhaps it was business travel. Or it might have been a long-awaited vacation. Regardless, you knew where you would begin the journey and likely had a good idea of where you were headed. Even if you were visiting a place you had been countless times, you still probably engaged in some level of preparation. For a business trip, did you confirm meeting arrangements, flight schedules, and hotel accommodations? Maybe you made sure you had necessary files. You knew your game plan before you walked out the door. For a vacation, how far ahead did you plan? You might have researched the destination and gathered the appropriate wardrobe and essentials. While your level of preparation may differ, regardless of where you are headed, it is still necessary for a successful journey.

Even with great planning, you most likely recognize that only a portion of every trip is fully within your control. Additional aspects of the journey require partnership with others. A few elements may simply be outside your control. Yet by learning how to manage each of those, the seasoned traveler successfully reaches their destination.

The journey of leadership is similar in many ways. Each leadership role you hold represents a new excursion. Some challenges will be familiar. Others will be unique. Some you can manage easily on your own. Even more require collaboration and interaction with team members and colleagues at various levels.

This journey begins by focusing on the benefits of curiosity. There is much to learn about your work environment, your boss, or team members you oversee. Think you already know it all? Surprise! A strong start to every leadership journey begins with a sense of discovery. The things that have worked thus far may not be as effective moving forward. Embracing curiosity will help you gain greater self-awareness. You might even develop an understanding of why you do what you do (or don't do) and how you are perceived. Add in a measure of intention to learn more and focus on controlling truly the only thing you can control—yourself—and you are on your way.

There are three things that form the essence of this idea of discovery. First, understand how you come across to others. Second, recognize how your action or inaction affects your peers and team members. Finally, know how to close the gap between intention and perception. Approaching your work with a spirit of discovery creates opportunities to accomplish these goals. If you're feeling road weary and battle hardened, try opening yourself to discovery and wonder. If you spend time around children, you will quickly notice that they tend to ask a lot of questions. As a result, they learn. Adults, though, are typically less inclined to be actively curious. For most, curiosity becomes more of an internal process. You may wonder about something, but having answers is rewarded more than asking questions. This is especially true for leaders in most work environments.

You have risen to this level in your career because you have answers and insights that are valued in your organization, industry, and profession. The challenge is that leaders begin to believe they *must* have the answers. Even if they're curious about something, they might no longer ask questions (except statements in the form of a question, e.g., "You agree, don't you?"). Imagine what you may be missing by not actively seeking new perspectives.

THE BUSINESS CASE FOR CURIOSITY

Approaching your responsibilities with a spirit of discovery creates a mindset of learning that will help you accelerate success. This learning mindset can also cement your reputation as a go-to leader. Regularly practicing curiosity helps. When you treat curiosity like a muscle and continue to exercise it, you benefit in many ways.

Consider Sam. When he accepted his first executive role, Sam looked forward to making a positive difference in a new organization that had quality products and appeared to be on the verge of dynamic growth. The CEO expressed how excited the company was to have someone of Sam's caliber on the team. Several of his colleagues voiced expectations that he would make a real difference in the aggressive goals they had set for the year. Much was riding on Sam's shoulders, and he felt it.

After several weeks, another vice president, Mike, asked Sam for advice on a tricky issue involving a team member. Sam had significant experience with the issue in prior roles. Mike anticipated a difficult conversation that he wasn't looking forward to. Though he had limited information, Sam immediately "knew" what needed to be done. He made a few suggestions. Mike then opened the door for further assistance. Sam gladly put on his red hero cape and came to the rescue. He even offered to speak with Barbara, one of Mike's direct reports, about the issue. By swooping in and helping Mike, Sam thought he could score a quick win with a new and valued peer.

That's how Sam found himself sitting across from Barbara. Sam and Barbara had met a few times, but didn't have a working relationship yet. Barbara was clearly wondering why Sam had scheduled the meeting. As he sat there, Sam realized he had committed to address a problem when he didn't have all the facts. However, he had promised to share his experience and jumped in with little prelude. The conversation didn't go well. Further, Barbara later went to Mike to complain about what Sam had said to her. Mike took the position that Sam was out of line, despite having earlier indicated his agreement with Sam's recommended approach. Relations between their two departments took a downward slide. Barbara, who was well liked within the company, began mentioning to colleagues that Sam was an arrogant jerk.

A SPIRIT OF DISCOVERY

Frustrated and angry about being "set up," it took some time before Sam accepted that it was going to take significant work on his part to rebuild trust with Mike and his team. In the meantime, Sam's own team began to grumble because many of them were friends with Barbara. As relationships spiraled downhill, Sam wondered if he could succeed. It seemed that so many people were against him. Only later did Sam reflect on his role in the situation. He realized he had been too caught up in trying to impress everyone with his knowledge and experience when he should have asked questions to learn more. Rather than jumping in to fix things himself, Sam could have offered only what he was asked for—his ideas—and left it at that. He could have queried Mike to learn more. The questions might even have helped Mike find his own solution. Curiosity matters.

Sam is not unique. When people are sure that they have the right answer, the tendency is to stop listening. They no longer explore, and they ignore any information that suggests a different outcome than the answer they have pre-determined. Sometimes they may even be solving the wrong problem. This is a common human response. It takes thoughtful intention to remain open and curious. When you do so, it creates an opportunity to discover important facts. The facts can help you move rapidly up the learning curve to build relationships, motivate your team, and continue to grow your career. Many leaders understand the importance of asking questions to build trust, but there are additional benefits. Leaders who exhibit curiosity are generally perceived to be more effective. Those leaders enjoy greater engagement and stronger performance from team members.[1]

By now you have probably worked with leaders of both types: those who considered themselves the smartest in the room and, if you're lucky, those interested in others' perspectives. While both may have a clear vision of where they want to go, the latter invite discussion on how to get there. They listen to input and yet they still own the ultimate decision. Curious leaders recognize that they are likely to make better choices when they have improved access to information.

Which of those leaders would you rather work for? *Which would you rather be?* GPS highlights a path to be the kind of leader who inspires their team to achieve great success. Curiosity gets you thinking and encourages the same in your team members. It is enhanced by recognizing what might be getting in your way. Your competitive advantage becomes intellectual humility that feeds openness to new ideas and different perspectives. Getting there requires self-awareness, focus, and perhaps a dose of courage.

1.1: SELF-AWARENESS
(OR CHECK YOURSELF BEFORE YOU WRECK YOURSELF)

Self-awareness is one of the most important skills, if not *the* most important skill, for executive leaders. How well do you know yourself? How are you perceived in your new work setting? What changes would make you more effective? Do you have internal curiosity to understand your inner journey? Answering these questions will set you on the path to stronger, more successful leadership.

While most people think they are pretty self-aware, fewer than 15 percent really are.[2] Seeking to improve requires introspection and reflection, as well as the willingness to ask questions like, "What could I have done differently to get a better outcome?" We all have blind spots, even highly self-aware leaders. Blind spots are behaviors, situations, or triggers that you don't recognize but everyone else does. They can impact how you behave, what you believe, and the extent to which you react or respond to issues. What are yours? Hint: by definition, you probably don't know.

Lack of self-awareness kills curiosity.

Understanding that everyone has blind spots is a start. Don't be afraid to seek more information. This can help you avoid assumptions that might trip you up. Discovering a blind spot—whether on your own or with help—is a great thing. It represents an opportunity for continued improvement. You won't become self-aware overnight just because you decide it would be a good idea. There are, however, things you can do to increase your awareness. This might include actively considering:

- How you are perceived;
- Where you get in your own way;
- What you might do in a particular setting to get the best possible outcomes; and
- Who are your advocates, adversaries, and stakeholders.

Keep in mind that what works in one organizational culture will not necessarily translate to another. Every journey is unique. As you become more self-aware, you will understand how you impact your current work environment. You will also learn how you are seen in interactions with colleagues. Discover where changes on your part can supercharge your efforts. These insights can help you stay on track.

TAKE ACTION

1. It's comforting to think of ourselves as always being right; however, growth happens when we consider our contribution to negative results. It is tempting to look for causes elsewhere when solving for disappointing outcomes, but the silver lining is that these situations present personalized teachable moments. Starting with yourself begins where you have the most control. When a meeting or conversation doesn't have the outcome you hoped for, ask yourself: What was my role in the way things went? What could I have done differently? When meetings or conversations go well, what did I do that made a difference? How do these interactions compare with those in past organizations or on prior teams? Even if your intentions are good, you may not be having the desired impact. Rather than blame others, reflect on your behavior and contribution to success or failure. Be open and curious so that you become even better.

2. Have you ever taken a 360-degree feedback assessment? These tools, which measure a moment in time, compare your self-perception with input from your boss, peers, and direct

reports. If you are able to complete a formal 360, dig into the feedback. Even if you don't agree with what people said, what themes emerge that are applicable? What can you learn? Pick one thing to work on and apply it in your interactions for the next few weeks.

Seeking feedback for growth takes courage. If you don't have access to a 360 assessment, you can solicit the input of valued colleagues by asking them a few questions. This is simple and yet surprisingly difficult. Keep your questions straightforward and open-ended, such as:

- What's one thing I could do to help you be more successful? (which is about them)

- What's one thing I should do differently to be successful here? (which is about you)

Doing this well requires asking for insight and then listening without defending, justifying, or explaining. Think of it like internal market research. If what you hear disappoints you, take a deep breath and focus on how to reengage those colleagues. You need to know what people think in order to continue to grow and improve. Your colleagues already have a perspective about you, even if you are new to the organization. Asking gives you a peek into those perceptions. Sufficient ego-strength is necessary to hear and not react. Recognize that this is one piece of data, hear what they have to say, and then express appreciation for their time and contribution to your efforts to improve.

You may decide to send your questions via email or use a free online survey tool that will allow colleagues to respond anonymously. Seek input from at least a dozen people to help reduce any unconscious bias that one individual might reflect in their answers. Whichever method you use to seek insight, be sure to thank your colleagues for their ideas, input, and observations, regardless of how you feel about what they said.

1.2: MAKE SURE YOU DON'T TRIP ALONG THE PATH

Sam created a problem for himself because he wanted to impress his new colleague, Mike. He genuinely thought he had the perfect answer because he prided himself on being solution-focused. Unfortunately, he didn't ask questions but instead jumped straight to the remedy. He went overboard in seeking to prove his value. If Sam was honest, he also felt a certain level of control in guiding the issue because of past experience. However, he didn't have all the facts, wasn't familiar with the organizational culture, and volunteered to address a problem that wasn't his to solve.

Often FOPO (fear of other people's opinions) can cause leaders to behave in ways that they might not otherwise. This is particularly true when you are in a higher-level or highly visible position or are new to an organization. You may feel pressure (often self-imposed) to deliver immediate results, regardless of whether the results are yours to deliver or not. Though Mike was receptive to assistance, Sam could have easily asked more questions to learn about the issue with Barbara. He could

A SPIRIT OF DISCOVERY

have shared his relevant experiences with Mike and offered to be available if Mike wanted to talk further.

Cultivating self-awareness can help you understand where you may be getting in your own way. Think of it as checking that your shoelaces are tied so that you don't stumble as you walk along. There is value in balancing discovery and expertise. You bring useful experience to the table. A spirit of discovery will expand your understanding of the current situation. Think about when you travel to a new destination. You may feel confident in where you are headed, but at some point, you probably need to stop and ask for directions or information. Maybe you have to inquire about operating hours or request an appointment.

Similarly, in work settings, balance between inquiry and direction is needed. When you are in situations where you feel you must prove yourself, it can be particularly challenging to slow down and activate your curiosity. Even without those constraints, many leaders tend to spend more time making statements than asking questions. Are you one of those leaders? Could this be a habit you consciously need to address? Perhaps it's a blind spot. This is not a binary choice: either seek information or give direction. Successful leadership requires skilled use of both questions and answers—often in combination.

Further, pay attention to whether your questions increase your knowledge or if you are asking questions to prove you are right. If you work too hard to be right, no one will expend the energy to present alternative points of view.

Sometimes being right is the best call. Yet consider what you miss when your primary goal is being the person with all the answers.

There are many different approaches to leadership. Think about four possibilities based solely on actions that are high or low on directive and inquisitive behavior:

- support (low ask/low tell)
- direct (low ask/high tell)
- guide (high ask/high tell)
- discover (high ask/low tell)

Do you tend to direct or discover more frequently? When are you most comfortable telling or asking? Sometimes it is important to do both, and other times it is better to do little of either. Strength in one or the other of these styles without balance may feel comfortable but can create issues.

Each of the four approaches can be effective when used in the right situation. Note, however, that the things you value tend to drive where you place your time, focus, and effort. If you pride yourself on having answers, as Sam did, you may overuse that skill and be highly directive. Consider how this can influence whether or not you exercise curiosity.

Maybe you've heard the saying before that someone is "often wrong, but never in doubt." Lack of self-awareness kills curiosity. We all need a certain amount of confidence to get through the challenges of the leadership journey. Yet that should be tempered with realism. Having insight into how

Four Approaches to Leadership

DISCOVER (High Ask/Low Tell)

PROS:
Encourages open communication and accountability
Creates learning opportunities for all parties
Empowers others to grow and develop

CONS:
Can be seen as an interrogator
Sometimes people simply don't know what to do

GUIDE (High Ask/High Tell)

PROS:
Makes suggestions regarding direction/next steps
Questions strategies and thought process to help strengthen decision-making

CONS:
Between all the questions and all the advice, can be viewed as a micromanager

SUPPORT (Low Ask/Low Tell)

PROS:
Assures access to resources
Allows autonomy in goal-setting and work completion
Celebrates success

CONS:
Could be considered absent

DIRECT (Low Ask/High Tell)

PROS:
Provides clear, unbiased advice
When asked for input, gives specific direction
Applies experience in useful ways

CONS:
May be overly controlling

← MORE ASKING   MORE TELLING →

you are perceived and feedback on where you can improve is useful. Otherwise, optimism bias—the belief that you are better at certain things than you really are (i.e., "No problem. I've got this.")—can be compounded by the very real, human tendency toward seeking only information that supports your current view.[3] By focusing only on proof of what you already believe, you reinforce blind spots and gaps that may cause you, and others, to trip along the path.

TAKE ACTION

1. For one day, track how much time you spend exercising each of the four approaches to leadership and think about the following questions.

- Where are you most comfortable?

- Which approach do you favor when under pressure?

- Are you aware of when you engage in one behavior or another?

- How can you be sure which approach is appropriate in the moment?

- As you pay more attention to your behavior, what are you learning about yourself?

2. Start-stop-continue exercises are great for planning and continuous improvement purposes. A similar practice can be applied for personal professional development.

- Where do you consistently run into challenges?

- What one thing could you start doing that would make a positive difference?

- What one thing could you stop doing that would make a positive difference?

- What one thing could you continue doing to make a positive difference?

- Why haven't you made the change yet (really)?

- What do you need to do to get out of your own way?

This exercise expands on the reflection exercise that encouraged thinking about your contribution to situations that don't go well (section 1.1, Take Action #1). It's another activity where insight from those who know you well is beneficial and is also something you can do on your own.

1.3: LET GO OF THE NEED TO BE THE SMARTEST PERSON IN THE ROOM

You've been successful up to this point in your career and plan to continue to achieve success. Like most leaders, you've probably accomplished a great deal in spite of certain behaviors, not because of them. As leaders rise in organizations, it is important that they surround themselves with talented people and listen to the wisdom in the room. Too much self-reliance may feel like greater control over your destiny; however, such behavior can limit your potential. Discovering a better path forward may be the greatest gift of expanding your curiosity. Yet doing so can be challenging. If you want to continue to excel, you need sufficient strength to hear things about yourself that represent others' perspectives of you. This could be termed intellectual humility and recognizes that others may have beneficial insights, information, and solutions that you are not aware of or have overlooked. What might this look like in your interactions with others?

Confidence has probably played a large role in your professional success to this point. Your willingness to trust your instincts, take calculated risks, and rely on yourself has paid off. These successes, though, can lead to overconfidence. Perhaps your confidence is based on an impressive set of wins, of which you are understandably proud. Maybe you have a quick mind and easily see solutions. Regardless, confidence plays into certainty. It feeds the belief that we are correct in our thinking and actions. Rather than confirming we have all the facts, we begin to lock in on our view, as we saw in Sam's story. Many brilliant thinkers have observed that good decisions come from experience, and experience comes from bad decisions. Where have you made bad decisions? What have you learned from them? Understanding how you get in your own way can lead to purposeful action. This will help you change your behavior for better results.

> *Confidence plays into certainty. It feeds the belief that we are correct in our thinking and actions. Rather than confirming we have all the facts, we begin to lock in on our view.*

A companion to confidence is humility. Humility requires enough ego-strength that you don't define yourself solely by your self-image. It requires the ability to reconsider your position and admit when you are wrong or don't have all the answers. Humility respects others' views even when you are confident (but not overconfident!) that you have the best answer. This means keeping an open mind and being willing to change your perspective. The first steps on the path of discovery focus on internal curiosity. Demonstrating intellectual humility and openness to new ideas are aspects of external curiosity.

External curiosity becomes key to success as you rise in organizations. Be aware of how past accomplishments may lock you into a comfort zone and reduce your willingness to try new ways of leading. Instead, you continue to do what has always worked. That's what you've been rewarded for, so why do anything differently? Fight complacency! When you are bound too closely to who you are now, it is difficult to reach your full potential. You might not even recognize who you could become next.

Openness to new ways of doing things is a commitment to the disciplined pursuit of continuous improvement. It may require moving outside of your comfort zone to turn up your curiosity. Ask questions to learn, not to prove that you are right. Thoughtfully consider what you hear. This can help you develop yourself and your team and increase productivity. It is possible that your influence will also rise. This will be explored further in chapter 2. Here are a few recommendations to get started.

TAKE ACTION

1. Apply the "idiot test." We've already established that balance between telling and asking is helpful to good leadership. The types of questions you ask are equally significant. Questions beginning with "why" tend to make people defensive. Closed questions—that result in a yes or no or one-word response—will provide little data. Open-ended questions require more than a static response and are likely to help you gather much more useful information. Curious questions—how, what, and when—often produce the most thoughtful responses, though an exception is "what were you thinking?" Beware of rhetorical questions posing as open-ended questions. A rhetorical question is really a statement. If you aren't sure if a question is truly open-ended, there is a test you can use. Consider the question you plan to ask. Say the question to yourself and at the end, add "you idiot."[4]

Here's an example of how you might use this. The day before a Board meeting, you are reviewing a report when your project manager admits that additional information was overlooked. Further study is needed. This could change the recommendation to the Board. You are angry and frustrated but recall that you want to do more asking than telling. So you think of asking, "Why do you think I asked you to complete the analysis last week?" Now add the words "you idiot" at the end of the question. So, you are saying to yourself, "Why do you think I asked you to complete the analysis last week, you idiot?" If the question sounds natural with "you idiot" at the end, *don't ask it*. It is a statement, not a question.

Doing this can help you sidestep rhetorical imposters. Even better, consider holding your opinion for the moment. Turn on your curiosity and ask questions designed to help you learn more. If you feel it is important to share your perspective, do so without wrapping it in the form of a question. Clearly state your thoughts and then ask your curious question. It's important to recognize, though, that when leaders speak first, the leader's view impacts what others say. The result is that others may not share the rich insights you are seeking.

2. Practice discovery (high ask/low tell). When another leader or team member comes to you with a problem, it can be tempting to react as Sam did: to put on your red hero cape and come to the rescue. It takes wisdom and intention to set aside the solutions that come immediately to mind and seek to learn more. Doing so can help the other person better frame their issue. Often, they will solve their own problem and will appreciate your assistance, even if all you did was ask questions that helped them think differently.

To engage in discovery, let your colleague describe the problem and then brainstorm solutions. Ask them questions such as, "What would you do in this situation?" Help them think through possible options with questions such as, "How would that choice impact results?" or "Which option feels right to you? Why?" It may be difficult to avoid more directive behavior, particularly as your mind immediately identifies possible solutions. Manage your desire to take over. Your colleague or team member will often find it easier to realize their own answers when you serve as a sounding board rather than an adviser.

CHECK YOUR GPS

The skills discussed in this chapter serve as a packing list for your leadership journey. They are related to the **G** (Get Ready) in GPS.

- Reflect on your actions and their impact on others.
- Let go of the need to be the smartest person in the room.
- Approach interactions with team members to discover, not just direct.

Curiosity about yourself, your work, and your colleagues prepares you for the ongoing journey of leadership. A habit of introspection allows you to adjust along the way as you gather new insights and information. Leaders who stay curious are often better able to handle unexpected events because they have remained open to possibilities rather than being tied to a singular outcome. These practices can be enhanced by reflecting on your actions at the end of each day. Being self-reflective will lead to greater self-awareness. Being more self-aware increases problem-solving capabilities, memory, and ability to understand the feelings of another, among other things. It also decreases stress. Think through the day's events and interactions on your commute home or sit quietly in your office for a few minutes at day's end to make notes. Intentionally considering what went well and what could have gone better will help you play to your strengths and continue to improve.

You have been successful both because of what you have done previously and in spite of yourself. Don't get complacent. New situations require new ways of thinking. Self-awareness is necessary to recognize what's working and what you are doing that gets in your way. Only then can you determine where to adjust your approach. Regularly challenging your assumptions will keep you open to new possibilities. Curiosity can be incredibly powerful if you want to discover hidden truths and reveal blind spots. Open, curious questions are powerful tools. Engaging in more inquiry instead of consistently telling others what to do can increase your influence as you assist in others' growth. The impact you have on them multiplies your effect.

In her *Dialogue* of early letters, the 14th-century mystic Catherine of Siena compared the human soul to a tree. "What gives life to both the tree and its branches is its root, so long as that root is planted in the soil of humility." What might that look like, being "planted in the soil of humility"? Catherine suggested that humility comes from knowing one's self. Such self-awareness is enhanced by being grounded in reflection, letting go of being right, and expressing curiosity about others' views. For leaders, these are important concepts to remember and put into practice.

TRAVEL JOURNAL

As you think about your leadership journey, take a few minutes to consider:

- Which of the leadership behaviors addressed in this chapter are strengths for you and which signal potential for future growth?

- Reflect on the best and worst leaders you've known. How does the information in this chapter apply to them as models for the leader you want to be?

- Which of these concepts are most relevant to where you are now as a leader?

- How will you use the information in this chapter this week?

CHAPTER 2

Ask the Locals

"The difference between hearing and listening is comprehending. After all, knowledge is what you know, wisdom is acknowledging what you don't know." — GARY BURNISON, CEO, KORN FERRY

In chapter 1, you learned about tools and tactics designed to increase self-awareness. Now expand your inquiry to look beyond yourself to those you work with—the 'locals' on your team—and their points of view. Here you will explore the value that comes from hearing others' insights and seeking new perspectives. No one, individually, has all the answers. Especially at the executive level, you can be insulated from daily organizational reality. Shift toward thinking about how to access more, and better, information. Think of it like discovering an amazing new restaurant based on the recommendation of a local resident. Learning from colleagues with different functional responsibilities from your own can uncover new ways of thinking. Inviting contributions from team members who are working at a more detailed level can lead to great discoveries. Being intentional about gathering more insights will help you accelerate your learning curve, especially in new situations.

Continuing the theme of discovery, take a consultative approach that can help you gather alternative perspectives. Leaders can improve information flow by inviting ideas from others. Conversely, leaders can act in ways that shut others down. My grandmother used to say that we have two ears and one mouth for a reason, and they should be used in that proportion. But this is not a how-to treatise on listening. The goal is to excite your mind with the possibility of discovery that arises when you change your perspective.

You want to be the go-to leader who delivers results and inspires the team, right? Consider how *you* can improve as you commit to control your confident contributions. It may seem odd, but focusing on your own behavior can put others first. The simple act of stepping back for a moment can open the door to information and connection. This is simple, but not easy. If you can do it, it is the secret sauce to make you smarter, more effective in your role, and create opportunity for others to learn as well.

Leaders can improve information flow by inviting ideas from others. Conversely, leaders can act in ways that shut others down.

THE BUSINESS CASE FOR PERSPECTIVE-TAKING

Amara was second-in-command for the largest business unit of a successful organization with more than a century of history. In this role for just over a year, she was proud of what she had accomplished in her career. She hoped to one day be selected to run the business unit. Amara was regularly lauded for her ability to deliver results, but had recently run into roadblocks. Her work environment was feeling increasingly toxic, for both Amara and her team.

Most people have experienced this at some point in their career—a team discussion where folks are digging in on their position, sure that they are right. Perhaps colleagues are waiting for their turn to speak, not to engage in dialogue, but eager to share *their* answer as *the* answer. Amara was frustrated with her colleagues because that's exactly the behavior she saw. They were spending more time positioning around who was right than working together. Things took an uncomfortable turn when Amara was singled out as part of the problem.

In a key meeting, Amara was blindsided by analysis that her colleagues presented. The additional information changed the viability of a business deal she was advocating. She inquired about why she hadn't been informed, and they observed that she had access to the same information. Besides, she seemed to have already made up her mind and hadn't asked for their thoughts. It was an embarrassing oversight. She decided to talk with her boss about her concerns. When Amara expressed annoyance that her colleagues hadn't shared information more openly, she was shocked by her boss's response. Amara's boss felt that Amara was too focused on her own opinions. What? Because she lacked self-awareness, Amara saw this behavior as something everyone else exhibited, but didn't see it in herself. It was a particularly tough week for Amara. Though part of her felt crushed and unappreciated, she knew the only person she might truly control was herself. What could she do differently?

2.1: SHIFT YOUR POSITION, SHIFT YOUR VIEW

You have a ready source of wisdom available when you consider other points of view. Perspective-taking requires leaders to consider additional significant information, including colleagues' and subordinates' opinions, before they make a decision. Experience suggests that this may be the most important approach that authentic leaders take to influence engagement with colleagues and team members. Information often equals power. You essentially have an untapped information account to draw from when you purposefully look for views different from your own.

You have a ready source of wisdom available when you consider other points of view.

Think of it this way. Many data elements inform an important decision. Sometimes information is readily available, but for whatever reason, you don't see it. Maybe you saw the information but dismissed it. People's brains are built to anticipate and predict outcomes, so a human tendency is to pay attention only to information that confirms what is already believed to be true. This is confirmation bias in action.[1] In the same way, you and a colleague standing across the room from one another will likely see different colors if she holds up a multicolored beach ball. This is perspective. Your colleague might say that the ball is yellow, white, and red. You, standing on the other side of the ball, might disagree. It is red, blue, and green from your perspective. Both certain you are right, neither of you has considered if you have the full picture.

If your colleague is curious enough to ask you what your conclusion is based on, you might invite her to stand beside you where she would see that there are additional colors. While this is a simplistic description of perspective-taking, consider the times you have been confident of something. Maybe, like Amara, you were pushing hard for a decision, only to be surprised to discover new information that changed the outlook. The information isn't really new. It was there all along, obscured by lack of curiosity and awareness. There are limitations to any one perspective. Being open to a particular outcome without closing the door on new information can expand your thinking.

The value of curiosity and humility was mentioned in the first chapter. You may recall that humility, especially as applied to leaders, requires that you objectively step beyond your ego and seek more information. You might even actively seek to be proven wrong. Perhaps you have risen through the ranks because you are bright and see solutions quickly. It becomes easy to have confidence in your own thinking. After all, it got you where you are today. Intellectual humility represents your acceptance of the idea that things you *know* to be true might be wrong. Changing your perspective out of curiosity helps you continue to increase your knowledge and understanding. It has the added advantage of opening you to different ways to thinking. This personal sense of possibility can be a tremendous boon to success in the workplace.

TAKE ACTION

1. Whenever you find yourself feeling certain, stop and reflect on why you *know* you are on the right path. It feels good to be right, doesn't it? Let go of your certainty for a moment and ask someone else, "You have expertise in this area. What am I missing?" This question—and the assumption that there is always something you might have overlooked—opens the door for you to discover additional, relevant information. Asking is also a great way to make it safe for your team to comment on an idea and help fill in the gaps.

Equally useful are questions such as "How would you do this?" and "What challenges has the company encountered with this issue before (or what solutions have been tried)?" Even beyond your immediate team, consider who can help you tackle a problem. Does anyone have prior experience in this area? Who in the organization do you consider an expert on this topic? These questions can help you gain history and insight, particularly if you are new to an organization or managing expanded responsibilities.

2. You may have impeccable attention to detail and never miss the little things. Yet, what are you dismissing as unimportant that may answer a question? Here's a fun exercise to demonstrate this point. Count the number of **F**'s in the following statement:

"Moving fast as a result of changing demands is a fact of life in today's world. This requires of leaders that we also frequently pause and reflect to stay on course."

How many did you count?* Our brains, which are weighted to logic, tend to hear the phonetic sound "ov" when reading the word "of." We also unconsciously skip over words like "of," "the," and "and" that don't necessarily change the context or meaning of a sentence. These words seem unimportant. In your certainty, how often do you dismiss or discount information or ideas that seem unimportant but may be worth a closer look?

> *There are eight (8) f's. Most people get 3 easily and possibly 5, but many miss the "f" in "of."*

2.2: LET GO OF THE PAST
(FEEDBACK AND FEEDFORWARD)

Leaders are often tempted to talk too much because they want to influence or persuade others. Influence requires insight as a foundation. Try as you might to control others, the only person you can actually control is yourself. While you may not immediately agree with that statement, you will likely agree that you cannot control or change the past. What has happened is done. Opportunities to differentiate yourself, make amends, or impress others are in your future. Let go of the past. Focus forward and shift your perspective to gather more information.

One form of perspective-seeking is to ask others for their thoughts on what you can do differently. Warren Buffett has named two characteristics that may be the strongest indicator of good leadership. They are:

- actively seeking feedback and
- openness to what you hear.

Amara ultimately decided to work on her interpersonal relationships with colleagues. She hoped to serve as an example of how they could all work more productively together. She wondered about her blind spots and wanted to improve. Her first step was to actively seek input and ideas from her coworkers.

While Amara had often sought out feedback from mentors early in her career, once she reached the executive ranks, she rarely did so. This is not unusual. For most people, as we age and gain experience, the practice of seeking feedback declines. Less seasoned workers tend to ask for and act on feedback more often. However, in a study by leadership consultants Zenger Folkman of 63,000 leaders, those who continued to ask for and act on feedback, regardless of age and time in their position, persisted in growth and performance. They also tended to be perceived as stronger leaders.

As awkward as it felt initially, Amara resolved to hear what colleagues had to say. Regardless of what was said, she committed to saying thank you. This was difficult, especially at first. Amara's go-to reaction was to explain, persuade, inform, and otherwise dominate the conversation. However, she discovered that there was an inherent superpower in muting herself.

ASK THE LOCALS

Some colleagues wanted to catalog Amara's past sins instead of providing suggestions for how she could improve. She could have argued with them or tried to persuade them of a different view. Instead, she consciously chose to listen to what they had to say. Amara understood that she couldn't alter the past. However, with greater awareness and a commitment to change herself, she might change the future. She sought responses to the question, "What can I do differently?" She stayed open to the possibilities. From these conversations, she received tremendous insight. Two particularly challenging colleagues even commended Amara for seeking their input and expressed appreciation that she really listened to them.[2]

Asking for thoughts on where you can improve does not cause people to form impressions of you. They already think whatever they think about you. Asking, though, benefits you. It opens the door to information that can help you identify potential blind spots and generate greater self-awareness. What perceptions do others hold about you that would be helpful for you to know? How might that increase your influence and positive impact on results? What can you do differently to be a better leader?

Others often see ineffective things leaders do or things their leader missed doing before the leader sees them. Get into discovery mode and ask. Then mute yourself. Don't react, justify, or argue. Listen to what they say. Even better, write it down. Then thank them for giving you something to think about, and go reflect on what you heard. Focus on the feedback that was most surprising or where you have the most disagreement. Maybe the comments will immediately resonate. Perhaps the response is more about the other person than it is about you. Regardless, what can you learn from their perspective?

The key to this approach is a specific focus on the future. It is "feedforward," a term envisioned by leadership experts Marshall Goldsmith and Jon Katzenbach that emphasizes prospective action.[3] Marshall Goldsmith has observed the common experience of having a friend, significant other, or spouse share their carefully collected and meticulously managed records of past errors and deficiencies. How useful is that? When it happens to you, are you impressed with their brilliant memory? Probably not. When others have a difficult time letting go of the past, creating a habit of asking what you can do differently going forward may help. No one can change the past. But when you focus on the future, it opens up opportunities for change and allows you to build on success. Actively exercising your curiosity will help you collect ideas. Silencing your desire to reflexively respond will increase the chance that you'll hear themes that can benefit your career growth.

TAKE ACTION

1. Proactively look for input and insight rather than giving it. As you receive forward-looking advice, how will you capture what you've heard? It's too easy to say, "I'll remember." Be sure to write it down. Taking notes has two benefits. You capture the information on paper, in the moment. Additionally,

writing signals to your brain that this is important. It helps imprint the suggestions in your memory.

While the terms *feedback* and *feedforward* may be used almost synonymously here, asking for ongoing suggestions for the future is different from asking for feedback. Feedback is about how you have done in the past. Some people won't tell you where you have screwed up, especially if they are conflict avoidant. Those at lower levels may simply be afraid to say what they think. Looking forward takes away some of that pressure. It isn't what you've done in the past but what you could do in the future that will make a difference. Suggestions for the future will help you better achieve positive change.

Practice listening intently and saying thanks, whether the person provides feedforward or feedback in response to your questions. Whatever they say is their perspective. Look for patterns or themes in the observations you receive. You may hear something similar from multiple people. Even if you don't agree with what is being said, write it down. Consider that you may not see or experience what they see and experience. Your perspectives are different. Listen without judgment. Not reacting or defending is key to being thoughtful in your consideration of the information you receive. Thank the person, and if the information was all backward-looking, perhaps ask, "Is there anything else you would like me to do differently in the next thirty days?" This emphasizes that you anticipate changing your behavior. Write down any suggestions they offer.

2. A colleague told me about an executive he admired as he was rising in his career. That leader would listen to subordinates' comments. Then, even if he might have a response in mind, would say, "You've given me a lot to think about," and would schedule time for a follow-up conversation. The colleague learned from working with that executive the importance of pausing and considering what you hear. Creating space between listening and commenting allows time to reflect on what was said. By not immediately reacting, team members felt heard, even when their ideas were not embraced. How can you use this concept in your work today?

2.3: SHUT UP AND LISTEN

Silence is a powerful tool. Being comfortable with silence creates space for others to talk. You may not even need to ask a question if you can resist the urge to speak long enough to see what else your colleague has to share. Maybe you are struggling with this idea of muting yourself. You earned a position of responsibility because of your knowledge, skills, and accomplishments. The team can benefit from what you have to share. Yet, if you truly want to be influential, get away from that constant need to inform, persuade, or demand. In her book *Conversational Intelligence*, Judith Glaser refers to this activity as "tell-sell-yell" behavior. Instead of being a "tell-sell-yeller," intentionally practice more listening.

ASK THE LOCALS

Being a good listener is much more than just keeping your mouth shut and nodding to show attention while others talk. The best listeners use questions to confirm their understanding of what has been said. They play back what they hear and ask for confirmation that they understand. In this way, leaders help team members and colleagues clarify their positions. Listening is not about silence but rather attention and the ability to ask thoughtful questions. However, use questions in moderation here. Filling silence with the sound of your voice can diminish your power.

Kate Murphy, author of *You're Not Listening*, has observed how some people are able to listen and entice others to share. Have you ever experienced a friend or family member telling someone else something you didn't know? This can happen when you stop being curious about what you know (or think you know). Maybe the other person asked good questions and didn't interrupt or judge. Remember, the human brain anticipates and forecasts outcomes as it sorts through information. As a result, you may hear only what you expect to hear, particularly with people and topics that are most familiar to you. That makes it even more important to listen carefully and then check your understanding with relevant questions.

In particular, exercise caution when dealing with issues arising from interactions based on experience—either with a certain person or past work experience—where you think you have a good sense of what's going on. Chances are, you've already passed judgment one way or the other. Leaders often assume they already know what the other person is saying. Because you are smart, experienced, and paid to find solutions, the tendency is to stop listening and let your mind jump ahead. It is challenging to listen non-judgmentally. When you're able to do it, though, you open yourself to new perspectives and broader vistas. You are also able to enter into more respectful, fair interactions. It requires awareness and intentional action—and is worth the effort.

TAKE ACTION

1. If you want someone's opinion, don't tell them yours first. Because of organizational power dynamics, once the leader speaks, others in the organization typically begin to position themselves relative to what the leader said. Do you want to learn more about what's going on in your organization? What specifically would be useful to understand? Who are key stakeholders who might share useful information? Asking open-ended questions rather than seeking yes or no responses is likely to yield more useful insights. Hint: refer back to the "idiot test" (section 1.3, Take Action #1) if you're tempted to ask rhetorical questions.

Practice silence balanced with relevant questions that deepen understanding. Approach meetings this week with a listening attitude. How long can you go in each meeting without saying anything? What do you learn that surprises you?

2. Seeking perspectives should be thought of as a two-step practice. First, ask for feedforward or insight into how you are perceived. Then stop talking and listen. Growing up, my mother forbid us from saying "Shut up." It was impolite and neither young ladies- nor gentlemen-in-the-making used

such language. Instead, we were to say, "Be quiet." Somehow the phrase "be quiet" doesn't seem to capture the strength of action needed for leaders to shift from a habit of telling to one of asking. Telling yourself to "shut up" is a deliberate pause to exercise the superpower of muting yourself. If you find yourself struggling with this practice, try posting the letters W.A.I.T. in a prominent spot in your office. This will serve as a reminder to ask yourself:

W.hy
A.m
I.
T.alking?

3. Dialogue is more about listening than anything. Your job as a leader includes helping others be heard. As you listen to team members, consider what the other person is saying and then play it back to them. What did you capture? What did you miss? Your playback can help them clarify their thinking.

CHECK YOUR GPS

Many experts have observed that, while it can be lonely at the top, it is difficult to succeed on your own. This is true of leading others and creating change within yourself. Open yourself to different ways of looking at old challenges. Actively seeking others' ideas about where you can grow and increasing how deeply you listen invites others to be part of your leadership journey. As mentioned in chapter 1, reflect on interactions and events at the end of each day. What worked well? What do you want to do differently tomorrow? As you continue to identify patterns and opportunities, you will advance on the path of leadership. In particular, think about these actions:

- Shift your perspective.
- Ask for ideas on how you can change moving forward.
- Consciously choose to listen more than you talk.

These behaviors serve as sign posts that support your ability to adjust on your path of leadership—the **P** (Pay Attention) in GPS. By practicing these techniques, you will demonstrate your curiosity and accelerate your learning around your role, team structure, or organization. Like Amara, you may initially feel awkward or silly seeking out others' opinions or insights as they pertain to you and the projects you are responsible for. In time, it will feel more natural.

Many leaders have reached their positions because they excel at the technical aspects of their job, yet the ability to manage the challenging people issues is where true leadership emerges. So let go of the need to be the expert and convert to listening mode. Displaying your expertise can be a difficult habit to break, but remember that most people are flattered when asked for their opinion. Team members may appreciate the opportunity to share with the boss what *they* know. When you give others the chance to shine and remain open to what they have to say, you stand to learn a lot about yourself (and probably them, too). Even if they never admit it, they will also recognize that it takes guts to ask.

TRAVEL JOURNAL

As you consider your leadership journey, take a few minutes to consider:

- What is the biggest challenge for you in seeking others' perspectives?

- How can you address that challenge so that you are more open to what you need to hear?

- Which of these concepts are most relevant to where you are now as a leader?

- How will you use the information in this chapter this week?

CHAPTER 3

Trust as a Bridge to Success

"Trust is the glue of life. It's the most essential ingredient in effective communication. It's the foundational principle that holds all relationships together."

— STEPHEN R. COVEY

Let's shift focus to thinking about how to bring out the best in others on the leadership journey. Achieving results through coworkers is a key aspect of success as you take on higher-level roles. How do you help team members and colleagues connect with their superpowers so that together you can build a super team? Your leadership will benefit from creating strong connections with colleagues and team members. Actions that build trust are a good place to start. Trusting relationships serve as a foundation for everything that comes after. The reliability, care, and consistency that is built over time reinforces the connection between colleagues. You know where you stand and whom you can depend on.

The ability to establish trust in work relationships is necessary for successful leadership. This is true for all leaders, perhaps especially those in a new role. People don't know you and you do not necessarily know the culture. Maybe you aren't new to your organization but have been promoted and now oversee the work of former peers. Reconfirming trust in these relationships is equally important. Or you have a new boss or new colleague and want to establish trust quickly to be more effective. You cannot force someone to trust you. It must be earned. But understanding what impacts trust, why it matters, and how to use this knowledge to further strengthen relationships can accelerate your success.

THE BUSINESS CASE FOR TRUST

Perhaps you've had this experience before: a work relationship that just doesn't feel right and yet you can't put your finger on what isn't working. Clare, an R&D executive, was running into issues with her new colleagues after joining a rapidly growing biotech company. The team had been excited when Clare accepted the position. Her expertise would help their pursuit of new product development. Yet there was something in her behavior that put people off. It didn't seem to fit well with the company's culture. On first impression, Clare was friendly and knowledgeable, but challenges quickly arose during interactions. People felt they couldn't trust her. An amiable bunch, they weren't able to clearly articulate what it was that made them suspect her motives. Sometimes they wondered if they were being too hard on her because she had a different style than most in the organization. As they worked to improve overall team dynamics, the real problem quickly became apparent. But before the riddle is solved, let's consider a few sign posts on the leadership journey.

3.1: THE COMPONENTS OF TRUST

Trust matters. Google studied their highest-performing teams and discovered that the best teams were built on trust.[1] What exactly does that look like? When trust is high, team members have confidence that they can take reasonable risks and not be punished. They are also more likely to seek feedback. This enhances performance and increases potential for innovation and continuous improvement. When trust is low, people are less likely to share their ideas or collaborate effectively. When work relationships are built on trust, companies tend to perform better over time. Research has shown that they outperform competitors that lack a culture of trust.[2]

Here is a simplistic and very real example. Have you ever played the survival game during a team-building offsite? There are many variations. The basic scenario is that participants have survived a plane crash in a remote wilderness area. They have a list of twelve items. Each item has been assigned a certain number of points toward survival. The number of points is not known by participants. Their job is to rank these items in order of importance for survival and identify how they would use each one. Every person does this individually at first. Then participants break into small groups. Group members bring their completed list and the group attempts to come to agreement. There is an element of competition as each small group tries to earn more points than other groups by identifying the items most likely to support their survival. When the activity is over, groups typically tend to score much higher than any individual. Debate, discussion, and sharing collective wisdom make a difference. That is the lesson of this exercise.

On an occasion that stands out in my memory, one group of executives went through this process and taught me another important lesson. When they were finished, they had the lowest group score of any of the others in the team-building session. At the same time, a member of their team had the highest individual score. He had expert knowledge that should have given the group an advantage. What happened? Based on prior interactions between the executives on this team, there was little trust. The individual who had expert insight was perceived as overly confident and dismissive of others. He often openly ridiculed their perspectives, even though he typically apologized later. In this case, his group felt empowered to disregard his input. He stopped sharing what he knew, almost in retribution. The group "perished," even though he had information that would have made a difference in the outcome of the game. How often does this happen at work? This is a simple but telling example of the consequences of low trust.

Increased performance resulting from trust reveals itself in many ways. Stanford Professor and author Robert Sutton has observed that there is significant evidence "when people argue in an atmosphere of mutual trust, that they're more likely to bring different perspectives. They're more likely to develop the best ideas."[3] You probably prefer that your team members don't argue, but this point about trust is worth considering. You won't always agree with others' perspectives at work. When there is trust, there is greater opportunity to disagree without being divisive. That allows continued dialogue to generate stronger solutions. Maybe disagreement among the troops makes you uncomfortable as their leader. Keep in mind that the further you are up the chain of command, the more information is filtered. When people feel safe to speak up because there is trust in the room, you are more likely to hear things you need to know.

Trust is an important element to bring out the best in your team, yet some conditions and contradictions exist. It is worth noting that even with an open, trust-filled culture, some team members still won't be comfortable speaking up. This can be due to culture or personality, no matter the tone of the organization. Group norms come into play. Your actions as a leader matter. What you do to increase trust, involve your team members, and draw out their perspectives will make a difference.

> *The more your actions suggest you are "all about me," the less trust there will be.*

When trust is not forthcoming, there are many ways to address the problem. There are five specific components I use with clients to diagnose and resolve the issues that emerge when there is a lack of trust among coworkers. Time and time again, I've seen how these concepts resonate with leaders. While many think they have a good gut sense about what impacts trust in their organization, considering each of these elements helps leaders dig deeper and assess what drives the degree of trust in a relationship. Understanding the levers and how your actions can influence each one can serve as a bright lamp in a dark forest.

Dependability is demonstrated by impeccable follow-through. Even the smallest promise matters. Let's say a colleague tells you they will send information before the end of the day. Then they head home without taking action. That will begin to degrade your view of how dependable they are. Their demonstrated commitment to their responsibilities increases your perception of their dependability.

Credibility represents confidence that the person has the expertise to do their job. Often credibility is based on past successes and credentials, but a sterling resumé alone is not sufficient. One impressive C-level leader I worked with often talked about the importance of leaders being upbeat. When his organization began to experience production difficulties, he ignored the problems. He instead took on the role of cheerleader. Unfortunately, he lost credibility with employees. Front-line workers were dealing with significant issues on a daily basis. They didn't need a pep talk. They were looking for someone to acknowledge their problems and provide a way forward. Leaders who are seen as credible know what they are talking about. They have the know-how to do the job, and they don't shy away from the real issues.

Care involves taking time to get to know one another. This requires demonstrating interest in and empathy for others.[4] What are their professional dreams? What are their biggest challenges? Kindness and curiosity strengthen relationships. Sometimes leaders feel they need to be all business so that they are well-regarded. However, the ability to thoughtfully engage allows leaders to establish strong bonds of trust with team members. Think about someone you know well. If they did something annoying, you might be more likely to excuse their poor behavior because you know them to be a good person. The same behavior from a stranger might be less forgivable. This is where care and presumed intention intersect.

Respect in this case is not something others earn, but rather something you express to them. How do you treat your team members and colleagues? If others come from a different culture, what does respect look like to them? Curiosity and openness to understanding their perspective on respect can be helpful. Even if you don't particularly like someone, you can still show respect. In fact, trust is not about likeability. By acknowledging each team member as a person, you honor the work relationship.

Intention reflects why you do or say the things you do. It represents the personal goals you bring to interactions and the perceived motives that others attribute to you. In many respects, intention may be the lever with the greatest potential impact on trust, either positive or negative. Perception is critical to this element, because it is the intention that others attribute to your actions that drives this element of trust. Communication can play a crucial role in helping others understand why you do or say the things you do. In the absence of understanding, they will draw conclusions. Maybe you're a quiet person who doesn't feel the need to share a lot of information. Are your motives clear? If people have to guess why you act in a certain way or what is behind the questions you ask—and they don't know you well—they may assume poor intent. You will have less impact as a result. While clarity of intention matters, ultimately the perception others have of you has the greatest influence on this factor. Keep in mind that the more your actions suggest you are "all about me," the less trust there will be.

Impact of Perceived Intentions on Trust

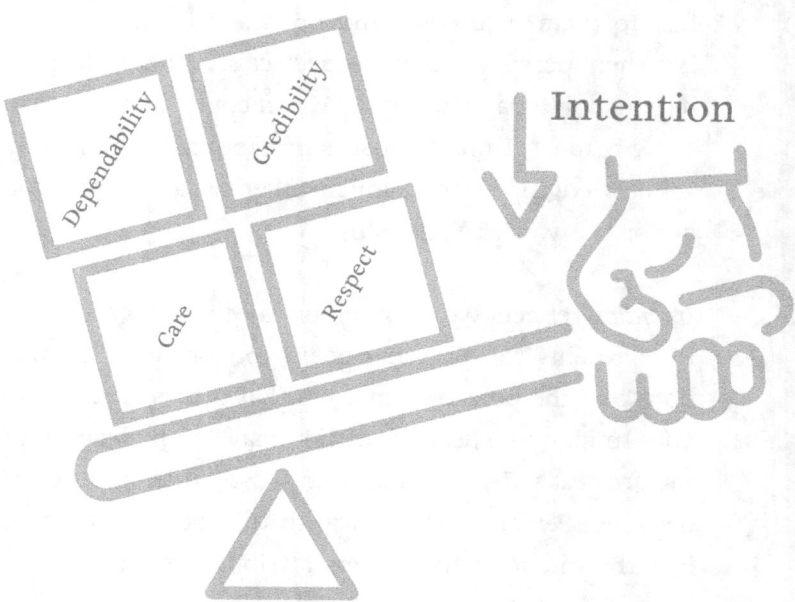

None of the five components of trust stand alone. They are interwoven with one another. The more you demonstrate dependability, credibility, care, and respect in interactions with other people, the easier it is to build trust. However, you must recognize that when motives are not clear, others' assumptions about your intentions can overshadow the other elements. This reduces overall trust regardless of the strength of dependability, credibility, care, and respect.

Unlike Clare, Mark was a sales and marketing executive who excelled at creating strong, trusting workplace relationships. This ability led to significant professional success for Mark and enhanced results for the organizations he served. No surprise, people wanted to work for him. Mark often talked with his team about the "bank of trust." This was a fundamental leadership principle for him. As he explained, it is important to regularly make deposits in this bank. Even the best leader is only human. At some point, whether intentional or not, all people make withdrawals from the bank of trust. When leaders act in ways that cause a withdrawal, it is important to acknowledge the error and apologize. If you have built up a sufficient balance in your trust account, your work relationships will remain intact. You will not be overdrawn.

The Bank of Trust[5]

Deposits	Withdrawals
• Sharing information transparently	• Misrepresentation of information
• Keeping commitments	• Breaking commitments
• Showing courtesy	• Acting disrespectfully
• Honoring confidences	• Gossiping and spreading rumors
• Curiosity and openness to feedback	• Ignoring input
• Clearly communicating expectations	• Undermining or blaming others
• Expressing appreciation	• Arrogance or disdain for others
• Acknowledging contributions	• Taking credit for successes
• Apologizing for missteps	• Defensiveness

TAKE ACTION

1. If you are trying to determine why there is struggle in a relationship, consider the components of trust. It's easy to get into a frame of mind that labels others as the problem. Start with yourself—and be honest. Are you holding yourself accountable for the same behavior you expect from others?

As you think about your interactions, the first question to ask yourself is, "Have I given up on this relationship?" If you have not and are willing to make changes, identify things you can do differently to improve your behavior and demonstrate dependability, credibility, care, and respect. You might also reflect on these questions:

- How are care and respect demonstrated in your interactions, even when the other person isn't reciprocating?

TRUST AS A BRIDGE TO SUCCESS

- What can you do to more clearly communicate your intentions?

- Thinking about the other person, what questions do you have about their credibility or dependability? If you are dealing with a credibility or dependability issue, focus on performance. Paint a picture of what is possible and then express curiosity to find out what's getting in the way.

- If you question a colleague's intentions, how can you learn more about them to understand where they are coming from?

To take this a step further, conduct a SWOT-like analysis of the relationship using a chart similar to the one below. For each component of trust, what are your strengths and weaknesses? Where are opportunities or threats to success?

Dependability Do what you say you will do	**Credibility** Understand the substance of subjects you discuss
Care Demonstrate empathy and interest in others	**Respect** Actions acknowledge humanity of others

Now examine intention. You may mean well and have honorable objectives. Typically, so do others. Are your motives clear? When self-interest is perceived as a primary driver of behavior, it resembles Pac-Man, eating up everything in its path. Self-serving intentions, whether real or imagined, often have the most detrimental impact on trust. As a starting point, you might note how often you say "I" versus "we" in work conversations. This can be a good indicator of your level of self-orientation compared to thinking about the team. Remember, "all about me" perceptions negatively impact efforts to improve and enhance dependability, credibility, care, and respect and, as a result, reduce trust. Whom do your actions serve? What do you need to do to adjust? How can you make your intentions clear?

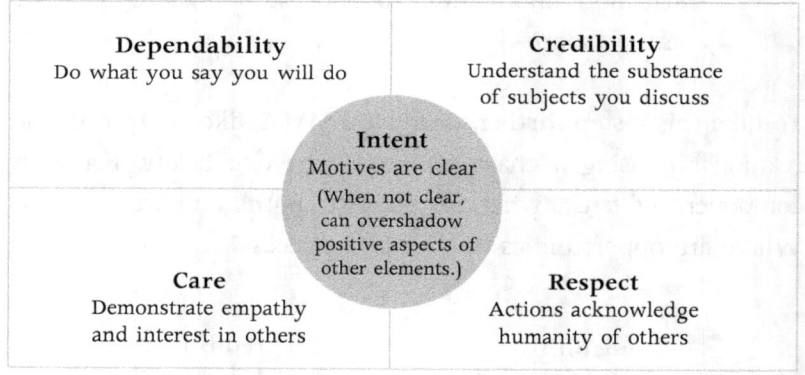

When thinking about those you don't trust, check the assumptions you've made about the other person's behavior. Are you acting on facts or on conclusions you've drawn that have raised doubts? If you aren't sure, you might describe to that person your expectations and the gap you see. Then ask, with genuine interest, what's going on. Be aware that if trust is low on their side, they will be less likely to risk sharing their perspective.

Whether you face an issue of earning others' trust or are engaged in diagnosing why trust is low with a colleague, the first step is to consider *your* behavior and *your* role in the situation. Often misunderstanding breeds mistrust on both sides. Ultimately you can't control what others think or what they do, only how you show up and interact with them.

2. If trust is low on a team, look first at your interactions as a leader. What are you doing that may create issues between team members? I know an executive who believed that stronger decisions came from asking more than one person to work on an issue. She would speak to each person separately so that they thought they had primary responsibility to drive toward a solution. When they learned others were "playing in their sandbox," it typically led to anger, frustration, division, and rivalry, not greater thinking. Clarity and consistency in communication are hallmarks of good leadership, as is transparency. Start with yourself to make sure you are not sowing seeds of distrust within your team.

3.2: TRANSPARENCY

Remember Clare? She was having trouble connecting in a meaningful way with her colleagues. She was frustrated. They were too. They questioned whether the right hire had been made for such a key role. There was a fundamental lack of trust. Further exploration of the team dynamics at the senior management level revealed that Clare was perceived as caring only about one thing: herself. She wanted to establish her credentials and impress her colleagues (i.e., add value). Her skills may have been exactly what the organization needed to move forward, but she had not spent time getting to know her coworkers. They felt dismissed and disregarded. Clare had not demonstrated interest in understanding their perspectives or contributions. Even though she was seen as credible and reliable, team members felt neither care nor respect from her during their interactions. As a result, Clare's motives were suspect. This impacted her ability to establish good working relationships that were built on a foundation of trust. What could she do to get back on track?

Transparency accelerates the process of building trust. What exactly is transparency? Clear communication and information sharing are key aspects. Connecting with the team in a way that helps them see how they are contributing to the bigger picture is also important. These actions increase the likelihood that you will be aligned on goals and moving in the same direction. Further, leaders must show realistic optimism about the future. They should set forth a clear plan for their teams to accomplish their goals. Those leaders bring their optimism and transparency to work on behalf of their teams. Clare may have been excited about the company's future and how she would contribute. Unfortunately, her approach to issues came across as self-centered. Quite simply, she wasn't seen as a team player.

If you are struggling with transparency, consider the components of trust. You can be knowledgeable, well informed, and bring great experiences to a project. That means you are credible. You may be doing exactly what you say you'll do. You are dependable. However, if your interactions with others lack care and respect, your ability to create productive relationships will suffer. People tend to excuse bad behavior from someone they know well. It is a human tendency to give them credit for good intentions. We tend not to do that with those we don't know. People who share their thoughts and intentions authentically are generally seen as more credible. Their messages are more often heard, and they are considered more trustworthy. It's hard to be transparent when trust has been damaged or hasn't yet been established.

Do you need to trust others first before you can be trusted? Whether intentional or not, people tend to give what they get. Sometimes referred to as social reciprocity, this behavior reflects what they feel they are receiving. It can be a helpful clue to where trust and transparency might be improved. When you do not trust others, you tend not to be as transparent. Things can easily spiral downward as a result. Your behavior can cause others to question your motives. Then the question of trust, or lack of it, becomes a self-fulfilling prophecy.

When people don't know you well, you haven't yet established trust, or trust has been damaged, interactions can take on a life (and story) of their own. Some people's natural tendency is to assume the worst. This is a human defense mechanism; it prepares us in case the worst occurs. If colleagues are drawing conclusions and creating stories, the stories are likely not positive. Further, people tend to decide what they think of you, based on your behavior, before they listen to what you have to say. Assumptions are made. Acting on assumptions results in reactions that confirm the story you've already told yourself. Your colleagues may be doing the same as they try to figure out where they stand with you. Transparent communication is both a skill and a mindset. Working relationships tend to improve through open, honest communication and behavior that supports an increase in trust.

Transparency and the development of trust go hand in hand. This may be because transparency—especially taking the time to share information and learn about others—demonstrates to team members that they are appreciated. Doing so gives you a chance as a leader to get to know the people you are working with. You can think of transparency as clear and open communication. Involving your team in creating a vision for the work all of you will do helps everybody feel like a vital part of the team. It creates greater connection to the work for everyone involved and leads to better performance overall.

TAKE ACTION

1. Engage with your team in conversations that allow you to get to know one another better. You can learn a lot about the skills at your disposal when you actively inquire about team members' backgrounds and contributions. These conversations also may open the door to reciprocal interest in you as a leader or colleague. Ask questions such as:

- What accomplishments are you most proud of?

- What strengths are you not currently using that you would like to use?

- What skills do you want to develop?

- What have you tried recently that didn't work out and what did you learn?

TRUST AS A BRIDGE TO SUCCESS

- How can I help you succeed (relative to responses)?

2. How can you increase transparency? Sometimes you have to explain why you are doing what you're doing, e.g., "I'm asking because...", rather than assuming that others understand your actions. Maybe you tend to think things through before talking to others. When you reach out to them, you might forget to properly frame the subject. It's like you had the conversation in your head and then brought others in midstream. Giving the "why" with the "what" adds meaning and context and demonstrates thoughtfulness.

Other ways to increase transparency include sharing information when you have it. Sharing information is one way you empower others. Don't assume everyone has the same insights you have. Ask open-ended questions to understand what is on their minds (see section 1.1 for examples). Even if the situation is developing and you don't have all the answers, you can let colleagues know what you can and can't share, and that, as things change, you will provide updates. Remember to follow through on those commitments.

CHECK YOUR GPS

Trust is a key building block in the foundation of positive, productive work relationships. You enhance the packing list for your leadership journey by being aware of the components of trust: dependability, credibility, care, respect, and intention. The benefits of transparency provide further insight. This understanding also serves as a sign post of where you are headed. It can help you identify when adjustments need to be made along the path.

In that way, trust and transparency are related to both your preparation and your flexibility on the path of leadership, the **G** (Get Ready) and the **P** (Pay Attention), respectively, in GPS. One of the fastest ways to create connection and alignment is to act transparently and communicate openly. This builds trust, yet it also requires awareness and balance among each of the trust components. Perhaps the strongest business case for trust is simple: your effectiveness and that of your team.

TRAVEL JOURNAL

As you think about your leadership journey, take a few minutes to consider:

- Which component of trust is the most challenging for you?

- Do you tend to trust too easily or to withhold trust? Whichever is your go-to approach, how has that impacted your work relationships?

- Which of these concepts are most relevant to where you are now as a leader?

- How will you use the information in this chapter this week?

CHAPTER 4:

Finding the Path Forward

"Leadership is about making others better as a result of your presence and making sure that impact lasts in your absence."

— SHERYL SANDBERG

As you increase your self-awareness, you will begin to foster additional skills that can elevate the performance of those around you. You have the ability to encourage greater trust within and among team members. Your actions set an example of what is and isn't acceptable behavior. Ideally, this includes understanding the importance of hearing others' perspectives. Success requires you to stay curious and not jump to conclusions. It means that you rise to the challenge of managing your emotions and not react to issues. These capabilities reflect your leadership presence and support your team members as they reach for amazing results.

In the last chapter, you explored why trust matters and the behaviors that impact trust. You learned how to use this knowledge to strengthen professional relationships. Continuing along the path, let's look at the actions you take as a leader. Your ability to control your emotions and keep communication channels open is key to being perceived as a good leader. Doing this well may require introspection to understand your personal hot buttons. What frustrates you more than anything? Why? How do you typically express that frustration? Knowing when you are on autopilot or reacting emotionally allows you to reset and thoughtfully respond. This will protect the investment you have made in professional relationships. Your ability to listen deeply and get to the heart of issues will help you bring candor to the workplace. Each of these tools is valuable for leading well in the moment. They will support your ability to find the best path forward on your leadership journey.

> *Your ability to control your emotions and keep communication channels open is key to being perceived as a good leader.*

THE BUSINESS CASE FOR PRESENCE

Leadership presence is often defined as the way a person carries himself, how she enters and commands the room, or the ability to engage confidently with colleagues to make a point. Now take a different view of leadership presence and think about it from an inside-out perspective. How can you manage yourself (inside) to achieve better results with others (outside)? The capacity to stay fully present and manage your reactions, even when others are losing their composure, is important. In the heat of the moment, it is fine to *have* emotions but you must work to not be *had* by them. The ability to match actions and intentions is essential. You must be aware of how you impact those around you. These skills allow leaders to find the best path forward for their teams and organizations. Leaders who have the ability to be flexible

FINDING THE PATH FORWARD

in responding to different situations further enhance their presence and self-management.

You may have experienced situations at work where a leader's lack of forethought created issues for an organization. People challenges can be compounded when leaders are too reactive. I experienced this with a CEO who became upset about the outcome of employee survey results we were reviewing. He and I had discussed the value of employees sharing their perspectives so that the senior team could continue to improve and evolve. Yet, he sought perfection. In particular, he was upset at the summary view of leadership expressed by the senior team. The less-than-perfect scores were a personal affront to him. Propelled by his anger, he barged into a staff meeting, visibly upset and waving the survey results. His question to staff was, "Who did *not* respond to this survey?" Interesting approach, I thought. Hands went up all around the room. Now, I knew that the response rate for that particular group had been over 80 percent. Clearly, they understood something that I did not. Self-preservation required that they pretend not to have participated. Then he wouldn't blame them for the result he clearly found unsatisfactory.

More examples of this CEO's reactivity began to come to light. Unfortunately, his behavior tended to shut people down. This prevented him from hearing things he needed to know to turn around a struggling company. Eventually the board of directors invited him to move on. He could have made positive changes if he had recognized how his reactions were closing off access to people and information. Fortunately, his successor possessed the skill to connect with people and invite their ideas. Getting to the crux of issues gave that person the ability to guide the organization toward greater opportunity.

Both CEOs had executive presence in the traditional sense. Only the second one had the leadership presence to respond thoughtfully and keep lines of communication open. He was able to connect with people, create trust, and get to the root cause of problems. The bottom line from exercising this soft skill was a significant improvement in product quality and market share.

A different path for many leaders is learning to respond, rather than react. Marcus, an Operations executive, ran into the challenges that being reactive can create. Normally a calm, steady influence, he was visibly upset after the company's CFO refused to approve more headcount for his department. Marcus had examined his budget and determined where he could limit spending to cover the cost of two more people. Still, the additional hires were being blocked, as all departments were asked to better manage fixed costs. Marcus was concerned that his team members were working day and night to meet their goals. Many had been traveling for months between company locations. They were tired, away from their families for extended periods, and working long hours. He worried that they would burn out or leave.

Marcus had been down this road before in previous roles where resources were tight. He was concerned that the CFO was oblivious to the long-term implications. His frustration reached the boiling point when he overheard the CFO tell his assistant to book first-class seats for an upcoming flight.

Then he learned that the CFO and another senior executive had played golf while on company business. The double standard for managing costs was enough to make Marcus's head explode. He approached the CFO at the coffee station with the intention of presenting a compelling case for headcount. Unfortunately, the situation escalated. Angry words were exchanged—all out in the open. It was uncomfortable for everyone, needless to say.

> *You can't control others, but you should be able to control yourself.*

Marcus was frustrated and angry. He felt the CFO was in the wrong, and yet knew that he had let his anger get the better of him. He decided to approach his colleague again, but only after he was more in control of his emotions so he could effectively respond with facts, not emotion. When the time came, Marcus talked about his commitment to managing fixed costs and how, in the long run, the additional headcount would be a cost savings. He learned that the CFO had prior experience with the Operations team padding their budget and was working from that frame of reference. Marcus was eventually able to get approval for the extra staff he needed. He also found out that the company had not paid for the golf outing. He was pleased when the CFO expressed concern about the perceived extravagance. Most significantly, Marcus felt that their relationship was stronger because he had practiced the inside-out aspects of leadership presence. He had reined in his emotions, considered how to align his words and actions, and listened to his colleague's perspective. Together, they found an agreeable solution. Marcus continued to exercise these skills. His ability to use these tools gained notice over time and his career continued to advance.

Events can trigger a reaction based on limited information or past experience. When leaders have an emotional reaction, they give up power over themselves. You can't control others, but you should be able to control yourself. This is not to suggest there's such a thing as perfect control or that you shouldn't show emotion. No one is perfect. Consistently work toward alignment of thought, emotion, intention, and result. That will demonstrate presence. It is okay to feel the emotion. How you act—the way you respond to inevitable challenges and disappointments—says volumes about your leadership. All of us can benefit from practice along the way. Seek to avoid drama, stay intentional with word and deed, and follow up on the impact of your actions. If you can do this consistently, it will build both trust and respect over time.

4.1: ALIGN YOUR WORDS AND ACTIONS

Your ability to connect, build trust, inspire action, and communicate effectively reflects your leadership presence. It starts with first impressions and continues beyond. Leadership presence, in this sense, includes the gift of engaging others through what you say and do. Think back to the components of trust (chapter 3). Those with strong leadership presence, as envisioned here, are not just credible and dependable. They do more than command attention. Their interactions show respect for others. They are in it for more than themselves. How do we know? They exhibit a certain relational transparency. Their warmth and respect come through in how their words and actions are aligned. This behavior leads to greater clarity.

By being more transparent, these leaders create a sense of "we're in this together" for their team. Their actions support their words. This alignment helps move team members away from uncertainty. It is easier for them to understand where they are headed. A lack of transparency from leadership often causes distrust. It may even reveal insecurity in the leader. Those perceived as withholding or hiding information that can help their colleagues may be seen as lacking confidence. This gets in the way of effective leadership. Knowledge and information often equal power. A willingness to share appropriately suggests that the leader has enough self-confidence to bring along team members. When your words and actions are aligned, this can fuel your presence as a leader.

If you want an aligned team, cultivate transparent, open communication in word and deed.

Think of it this way. People in authority influence what is and is not permissible in an organization. There is a saying that "a fish rots from the head." This is an apt metaphor for poor leadership. Your behavior sets an example that others follow, regardless of what you say. Lofty platitudes without action represent information, not transformation, for the organization. Leaders define the how, what, and why of behavior within an organization. There is the behavior you say you want and then there is the behavior that actually exists. The more overlap between the two, the better. In other words, the intersection of behavior that is encouraged and that which is tolerated is where transparency and alignment meet.

You create greater transparency when you are comfortable communicating the why behind your actions. The give-and-take in your relationships can enhance this clarity. You've learned how to be open to feedback. Your openness, in turn, can influence colleagues' positive perceptions of you. The key to cultivating good leadership presence begins with a recognition of your impact on others.

When Marcus realized how his emotions had negatively impacted the situation with his colleague, he knew he had to take a different approach. He demonstrated relational transparency by owning his mistakes, just as he would his successes. His actions encouraged the CFO to do the same. When leaders know themselves, it is easier to be internally aligned. Otherwise, you may confuse and frustrate those around you. The same goes for the rest of your team. Simply put, if you want an aligned team, cultivate transparent, open communication in word and deed. A leader cannot be effective when words and actions are not aligned.

TAKE ACTION

1. Why does clarity in your professional interactions matter? Here are some examples. You say that open, honest communication is important. Then you are overheard in the hallway

complaining about a colleague. Think about the message that sends. Or consider how organizations spend countless dollars on developmental training that prioritizes listening. Yet leaders continually interrupt one another and their team members. Their behavior reflects the true priority of listening to others.

- How aligned are your statements and actions?
- How aligned is your personal leadership?
- What do you need to do to be more intentional and thoughtful about your words and actions?
- When you are directing others, ask yourself if the same rules apply to you. If not, why not? Think about how this impacts your credibility.

Perhaps you've heard the question—or asked it yourself—"Why am I held to this standard when my boss, the CEO, or that senior executive over there isn't?" Lack of consistency between words and actions is a common contributor to reduced trust in organizations. Sometimes senior management follows a "do as I say, not as I do" philosophy. If you allow double standards in your interactions, you degrade trust and negatively impact morale. This reduces the potential for your team to achieve great results. It takes a strong ego and willingness to adjust, but as a leader, you set the tone. Be on the lookout for such inconsistencies and address them immediately. If you see lack of alignment at a higher pay grade than your own, consider what example you can set to reduce the negative impacts on your team's productivity.

2. Leadership presence isn't just what you know or how you show up. The way you interact with people is a contributing factor. How are you perceived? Ask people who know you well in work settings:

- How do you feel during our conversations? (This may seem rather touchy-feely but you can learn a lot from asking questions like this.)

- What is one thing you would like me to do to improve my communication skills?

- It is important to me to walk the talk. What is an example of where I do that well? How can I continue to improve?

4.2: BECOMING A CHAMPION LISTENER

Stephen R. Covey observed in his book *The 7 Habits of Highly Effective People* that "Most people don't listen with the intent to understand. They listen with the intent to reply." How many times have you spoken with someone who was so eager to respond that they interrupted you? What did they miss from what you had to say? How often are you guilty of this?

According to the National Center for Voice and Speech, the average American speaks at a rate of about 150 words per minute. However, people hear at a rate of roughly 1,000 words per minute. The gap between speaking and listening gives your mind a lot of extra time to wander. A wandering mind creates opportunity for you to miss important information, clues, and insights.

One of the best leaders I worked for during my years in corporate life was a senior executive named Fred. Fred was tough, but fair. When he met with you, he listened with intention and focus. While he was unwavering in his expectations of high performance, Fred was equally consistent in meeting the same standards he set for the senior leaders who reported to him. Fred wanted to hear where each leader was challenged and what solutions they had in mind. Working for Fred was rewarding because you knew where you stood and how to thrive. He taught me that there are potentially useful nuggets of information in any conversation. By exercising acute listening skills, Fred could understand and diagnose issues quickly when dealing with decision makers. His insights helped the team succeed. With Fred as a role model, I developed and refined communication tools that contributed to my success as a leader.

Listening to team members has proven to be more effective for achieving results than giving them feedback.

Taking in information is a key aspect of communication. In fact, intentional silence is a great way to become a better listener. Many leaders are guilty of what Marshall Goldsmith calls "adding too much value," among the twenty bad habits of leaders he explores in his book *What Got You Here*

Won't Get You There. Leaders who do this give in to the irresistible need to contribute their opinion and insights to every discussion. They are telling the world how smart they are at every turn. Instead, embrace and exercise the power of listening as a tool. Why? Listening to team members has proven to be more effective for achieving results than giving them feedback. Researchers have confirmed the link between good listening skills and positive perceptions of leaders. Those who listen well tend to have more trusting relationships with their teams. They are happier and more creative.[1] In short, good listening skills add momentum to your leadership journey.

TAKE ACTION

1. As you rise to higher-level leadership, good listening becomes more and more vital. There is a specific practice you may want to adopt on your leadership journey: as a leader, be the last to speak in meetings. This gives everyone a chance to be heard and allows you to gather new insights. It's important to recognize that once you speak, most people begin to position themselves in relation to your remarks. As previously mentioned, your comments as a leader can put boundaries on the conversation. Team members begin to work within those constraints. If you don't speak, there is a greater likelihood that the team will listen to and interact with one another. That's when great things can happen.[2]

The Dalai Lama is said to have observed, "When you talk you are only repeating what you already know. But if you listen, you may learn something new." For practice, don't say anything in at least one meeting next week. This may sound easy, but it can be challenging. It requires focused attention and listening closely to what is being said. Plan not to respond or engage in the discussion. Your eye contact and other body language will show that you are paying attention and actively engaged. Be open to what you hear without reacting. The question is one of efficiency versus effectiveness. It may be easier to tell people what to do; if you want compliance, perhaps that's the answer. However, if you are looking for alignment, let go of the reins. If you are successful in your silence, you may not need to say anything at all.

- How long are you able to go without speaking? Five minutes? Ten? The entire meeting? Try this at more than one meeting.

- Notice how others react to your silence. What do you learn that surprises you?

- When does it get easier to listen rather than talk?

A client tried this exercise over several meetings. He remarked on the difficulty he had not speaking up as his direct reports grappled with a problem. Eventually, they identified a solution he wouldn't necessarily have chosen; however, they were highly engaged and the end result was positive. The result demonstrated alignment. He was proud of controlling his urge to take over the meeting because his team was energized by their role in moving forward. His comments reinforced the idea that you might be surprised what you learn when you listen as much as—or more than—you talk.

COURAGEOUS CLARITY

2. Think you're a good listener? Have someone read the information below aloud to you. Listen carefully. Maybe make a few notes. Then answer the question at the end. Are you ready?

- You are the bus driver.
- You drive Route 1 and have seven stops before your break.
- At stop number 1, three people get on the bus, one of them wearing a red hat.
- At stop 2, four people get on and one gets off.
- At stop 3, two people get on, one person is carrying a bag, and the person with the red hat gets off.
- At stop 4, a group of seven schoolchildren get on and sit in the back of the bus.
- At stop 5, five more people get on the bus and two get off.
- At stop 6, no one is waiting for the bus and ten people get off, including the group of schoolchildren.
- At stop 7, a single passenger comes sprinting toward the bus only to learn that you are taking a break.

Here's the question: What is the bus driver's age?

Try this exercise with colleagues. How many of them answer the question correctly? The majority of people tend not to hear the first statement: "You are the bus driver." Why do you think that is? They miss the most important piece of information, which is that the bus driver's age is however old you are. While simplistic, this is a good example of how we tend to make snap judgments about what is and is not significant information. How often do you tune out on what someone is saying because of a similar judgment? What might you be missing?

4.3: WHEN STORIES TRIGGER US

In spite of all efforts, you may still run into rough patches. You seek to be transparent. You actively listen and connect with colleagues. At the same time, you're exhausted from working long days. Nothing has gone right this week. Expectations are high. Any of those impacts can weaken your ability to be more deliberate in responding to issues.

Human brains seek certainty to reduce fight-or-flight tendencies, attempting to determine if it is necessary to defend yourself or run when threatened. From an evolutionary standpoint, this was quite helpful and contributed to survival. In the modern world, it can get in the way. While certainty may make people feel safe, it can also cause problems. Employees crave certainty, while their leaders need to be comfortable with ambiguity. Certainty becomes a false comfort for leaders and may result in them misleading team members instead of addressing ambiguity, complexity, and the reality that not all things are known.

Further, in an effort to create certainty, people tend to string together assumptions and act on the conclusions drawn from experience. Sometimes they support their conclusions with a few facts for credibility. This tendency toward confirmation bias, referenced earlier in chapter 2, may cause leaders to seek to control situations to ensure specific outcomes. There is a common misconception about this perceived control. It is often seen as a positive attribute. However, the desire to control situations and outcomes can cause you to engage in manipulation. This isn't intentional. Rather, it is an unconscious attempt to reduce uncertainty for yourself and others.

> *It is much less expensive to push the pause button than to push reset.*

Before Marcus approached his colleague to discuss his concerns, he needed help separating the facts of the situation from his assumptions. Once he recognized how past experience was driving his expectations and behavior, he got his frustration under control. He began to acknowledge that he had reacted to a story he had imagined. That story became his hot button. Marshall Goldsmith refers to a hot button or behavioral trigger as "any stimulus that impacts our behavior."[3] Determining the events, interactions, and emotions that set you off might sound easy, but it isn't that simple. It requires developing greater awareness to admit when you might be telling yourself stories. You must become aware of your conclusions from the narrative you are creating and how it is influencing your behavior. As your awareness increases, you can be more intentional about how you respond—and not react—to events, people, and interactions. You can deliberately seek information that explores the story. Remember the power of asking, "What am I missing?" discussed in chapter 2. Doing this will help you manage emotions surrounding high-stakes issues.

A commitment to understanding the things that could spark a strong reaction will serve you well. It takes conscious effort to observe yourself with intention and become aware of when your fight-versus-flight response kicks in. What is the moment of impact? Think about how it feels to you physically. A former colleague's neck turns bright red when he is triggered. Some people don't have reactions that are as obvious to others. Maybe they inadvertently hold their breath or feel tension in their back, shoulders, or neck. Their heart races. They get a dry mouth, sweaty palms, or their body temperature rises noticeably. These signs alert them to the need to physically reset.

Paying attention to your body's response to a trigger allows you to recognize when the spark is about to become a flame. You can then pause and ask yourself, "Am I reacting to facts or a story I've created?" In the long run, the only thing anyone can control is themselves, their emotions, and their words. Reacting to others is not the best use of your time or energy. More importantly, when you react rather than respond to others, you give up your control to them. With practice, you can become more aware of assumptions and whether those beliefs are driving you more than you are driving them. Further, taking the time to understand facts and effectively respond is beneficial to your long-term success.

TAKE ACTION

1. Take some time. Thomas Jefferson supposedly said, "When angry count to ten before you speak. If very angry, count to one hundred." My mother had similar advice. She often counseled her children to "count to ten" before speaking or acting. When emotions are high, intentionally asking your brain to think about something else can short-circuit a tendency to react. This allows you to be more thoughtful. It reduces the likelihood that anger, frustration, or other emotions will hijack your thoughts, words, and actions. Try this the next time you feel yourself reacting to something. Take a deep breath and count backward or do a simple math problem in your head. If you are truly angry, be deliberate in pressing pause on a conversation. This allows you to get back on track. It is much less expensive, figuratively and literally, to push the pause button than to push reset.

2. Think before you react. Marcus had to separate the facts from the conclusions he was drawing based on past experience. This allowed him to control his frustration and avoid being triggered. He began to recognize when he might be reacting to something that felt real, but wasn't actually happening. This was a first step in moving toward being more intentional about how he responded to issues. There were times that he had incorrectly analyzed a situation that made him angry. He found that stopping to look for what he might have missed was helpful. Wondering why someone he otherwise respected was acting a certain way sometimes caused him to rethink his conclusions. Often, he would activate his curiosity and simply ask the other person what was going on.

Anyone can do this. You may not be as reactive as Marcus, but we all have triggers. There is a mindfulness practice known by the acronym STOP. It is a useful tool for creating a purposeful pause between reaction and response. This exercise can be helpful in raising awareness and creating a habit that will help you manage your triggers.

> **S** – Stop what you are doing. Be intentional in hesitating before moving forward.
> **T** – Take a breath. Focus on your breathing, in and out. Feel it as it enters and exits your body.
> **O** – Observe your breath, how your body feels, and any emotions or thoughts that are arising. Name them as you notice them. For example, you might observe that your shoulders and neck are tight, your hands closed, or you feel agitated.
> **P** – Proceed now that you have recognized what's going on with you physically and emotionally.

Sometimes taking a breath is enough to catch yourself before you react. At other times, you may decide to pause further or reconvene at a later time.

CHECK YOUR GPS

Pause, listen, respond. Your presence as a leader is more than how you command the room. It relates to your ability to align your words and actions. It is associated with your capacity to listen and leave space for others to share their ideas. What do you want to demonstrate through your actions? A conscious response to issues is more productive than jumping to conclusions and reacting out of emotion. These are tools that exceptional leaders manifest in their professional interactions. As sign posts, they reflect your ability to Pay Attention along the path of leadership, the **P** in GPS.

TRAVEL JOURNAL

As you think about your leadership journey, take a few minutes to consider:

- What is most challenging for you about listening with your full attention? What comes naturally?

- What physical reaction(s) do you have when you are triggered? Observe yourself this week and if it happens, pause and ask yourself, "Where do I feel or notice this in my body?"

- Are you reacting to facts or a story you've created? What if that story you've been telling yourself isn't true? How can you learn more?

- Which of these concepts are most relevant to where you are now as a leader?

- How will you use the information in this chapter this week?

CHAPTER 5

Managing the Inevitable Detour

"Every day you need to open the door for the next experience, rather than approaching life thinking that you know the answers."
— KATE JOHNSON, PRESIDENT, MICROSOFT U.S.

Let's face it, detours arise at some point in most journeys. You are under pressure to deliver results and yet sometimes you run into dead ends and derailers. It may seem that unexpected changes lurk around every corner. The reality is that leaders must learn to be fully present and engaged while also retaining enough flexibility to respond well to evolving circumstances. Understanding how to focus and prioritize can be beneficial to even the most seasoned leader. While you probably have a good idea of paths you might take, staying open and flexible to additional insights will benefit you and your team. How do you remain mindful, self-reflective, fully in the present, and still have a map of the future in mind to lead your team where it needs to go?

This chapter illustrates how the best leaders are able to balance openness and curiosity with delivering results to manage the inevitable detour. Most organizations want to give leaders time to grow and support their teams. Yet each one has goals to meet, products and services to launch, and customers to serve. Learning and insight often get pushed aside by urgent issues, even if the urgent issue is ultimately not that important. That's typically because it is easier to measure outputs (like products) than inputs (like thinking).

At the same time, there is a need to take in new information, develop relationships, and work collaboratively across functions. While you might want to focus entirely on what is directly in front of you, think of this as enjoying the scenery on a detour. You might be surprised by what you discover. If you are able to more consciously notice the surrounding environment, you can anticipate and avoid detours and obstacles in your path. The goal here is to remain open to new possibilities while not being distracted from key objectives. Flexibility, collaboration, and discernment are required.

THE BUSINESS CASE FOR IMPRESSING WITHOUT STRESSING

Alina was the new COO for a large regional bank. She prided herself on seeking feedback and delivering results. After holding the job for just over a year, she was frustrated when her boss said she was not achieving expected outcomes. She felt that she had made a tremendous effort to learn about her new environment; yet after an initial honeymoon period, her colleagues had disengaged.

Alina often jumped on the latest and greatest idea arising from her conversations. She loved diving more deeply into the details. Her boss suggested she was spinning her wheels. For someone who had delivered superb performance in prior roles,

MANAGING THE INEVITABLE DETOUR

Alina felt wounded by the comment. She had a strong desire to address the problem and was doing a good job of building relationships and coming up to speed on the organization's issues. Where she fell short was the need to consider how new insights fit with the valuable knowledge she brought to the role. Understanding that dynamic would help her determine the next steps. Unfortunately, her sensitivity, coupled with her desire to impress, pushed Alina into a cycle of reactive behavior rather than thoughtful response. She thought she was being open and flexible. Instead, she was caught in a whirlwind of short-term activity without focus on creating genuine momentum.

> *If reacting to problems is your superpower, are you sure you're working on the right problem?*

Talking to people, being open, and understanding yourself—these actions lay the foundation for the work to be done. They are not the work itself, but raw materials with which to build. Alina had to be intentional about slowing down to consider what she had learned in her time on the job; given *this* context, what does this situation mean and what are the possible outcomes? Pausing to reflect on where she had been made it possible for Alina to diagnose the point at which she'd gotten off track. To come up to speed, she had been busy gathering information. But individual points of data alone are not meaningful. She was confusing the means with the end. Recognizing themes and relationships gives data meaning. This realization helped her to discern where she should focus so that she could filter out the noise.

Your behavior, interactions, communication style, and body language all contribute to the image others have of you as a leader in the organization. Like Alina, you likely want to deliver great results. Being seen as a strong leader is important. Most people make quick judgments about others when they first meet. In every interaction, your reputation is being formed as your image develops. Self-awareness helps you understand how you are perceived. Similarly, the energy and enthusiasm you demonstrate for the team's success, not just your own, enhances how others see you.

In addition, your ability to engage others and become an effective facilitator of information is a required skill for a leader. Let's look at how learning to better observe what's happening around you and adjust accordingly can be beneficial to your leadership and your ability to collaborate productively with others. Don't let your desire to impress become an impediment. Unchecked, it can get in the way of recognizing how to thrive in spite of challenges you encounter.

5.1: THE POWER OF NOTICING

Improve your powers of observation and you will be better positioned to anticipate and address issues before they arise. The key to skillfully harnessing information to benefit yourself and your team requires integrity and curiosity. This can also help you prioritize where to place your time and attention. Some leaders struggle with noticing too much; others miss important cues. Alina's tendency to take in and process tremendous amounts of information had been a strength in the past. In her new role, as stress levels increased and information came fast and furious, it was too much. She suffered from what some call "dementia of the overwhelmed." This presents, in part, as an inability to stay focused and get things done. In Alina's case, she was driven by her desire to learn as much as possible in a short period and prove herself with an early win. Absorbed by distractions, Alina gave the appearance of being very busy, yet she was failing to make progress. To be successful, she had to tune in to the moments when she was losing focus or being reactive to information. Slowing down helped her become more thoughtful and more aware of what was occurring around her. She began to notice things she had been missing and could then decide where she might better place her focus and her time.

Randall, a tech company sales executive, also needed to work on his powers of observation, but for different reasons. He too was moving fast, although he tended to miss key details that others noticed. In Randall's case, his penchant for speed came across as "ready, fire, aim." This caused him to repeatedly miss his sales targets. Randall may have noticed things that needed his attention but he was caught in a flurry of activity that led nowhere. His lack of forethought and planning caused frustration and anger among his colleagues. His boss concluded that Randall was chasing the latest shiny object rather than being more strategic. Fairly quickly, Randall began to worry he wouldn't survive, much less thrive, in his role.

Whether you identify with Alina or with Randall or have a razor-sharp ability to focus, recognize that a variety of things can detract from your ability to notice what you need to know. Those who are highly perceptive tend to pick up on things that others completely miss. This is a great skill that contributes to anticipating and responding to issues. Yet this strength can be problematic if not managed. It is critical to apply your powers of observation effectively. Chapter 4 highlighted how successful leaders are aware of what's going on inside themselves. Those leaders control their emotions and reactivity to events and information. In addition, it is important to notice what is occurring around you, not just within yourself, and how you respond to those external forces.

People who are able to resist being overwhelmed by details often possess intuition. They may refer to it as "trusting their gut." They are able to perceive subtleties when interacting with others. Information is a tool for them to effectively determine how to move forward and how to partner with colleagues. This ability goes beyond knowing how to juggle a significant number of priorities. While you need to notice details in your work environment, you also need to observe people you work with and pay attention to what is going on with and between them. Leaders who are good at doing both can anticipate potential issues. Their ability to pay attention is an asset, not a distraction. They observe others and the situations they are in, then consider how to apply what they have learned.

So how can you improve balance in your powers of observation? First, be aware of what negatively impacts this ability for you. Undue amounts of stress can be as distracting for

MANAGING THE INEVITABLE DETOUR

some as a messy desk or too much electronic noise, such as the continual ping of incoming texts. Lack of self-care, including always putting others' interests ahead of your own, can also sap your energy and ability to notice key details. Whatever it is for you, distractions—including assumptions that pull you away from facts—may cause you to miss important clues about what's actually happening around you. Address the things that draw away your attention. Purposefully take time for quiet, thoughtful reflection. This can improve your outcomes and requires less energy than reacting to problems as they arise. Look beyond yourself to see what others do in your work environment. Pay attention to where issues arise. To get better at noticing, slow down, take a deep breath, and be more intentional in studying nonverbal cues and listening to what is being said.[1]

Such intentional practice often comes from training your mind to work in your best interests. There is a wealth of information available on meditation and contemplation. Being more in the moment can heighten your ability to notice information that will make a difference. Recognizing when you are being triggered (as described in chapter 4) allows you to stop reacting to the narrative in your head and respond more thoughtfully to facts. As you move beyond what is going on inside you, you'll develop clearer perceptions of undercurrents that are impacting others. You might deliberately and thoughtfully cultivate greater social awareness, empathy, and organizational awareness. Doing so builds resilience and expands your leadership, further supporting your ability to respond productively to detours and unexpected events.[2]

Some leaders become so lost in the inner dialogue with themselves that they don't notice important things going on around them. This can be especially true for leaders taking on greater responsibility, particularly when you are being bombarded with information and significant demands. And it can happen without you even realizing it. The more you can pay attention to things other than yourself, the more compelling you will be. Be careful, however, not to fill in knowledge gaps with assumptions based on prior experiences that are not applicable to the current situation. As you gather new insights, rather than assuming you understand or can figure things out on your own, ask questions to test your theories and learn more. Really listen to what is being said. Dig deeper if necessary, not to argue or persuade, but to learn and clarify.

On the opposite end of the noticing spectrum, you may have a challenge more similar to Randall's. Are you often distracted by external demands and details? Do you find it hard to get things done because of all those distractions? Think of the bouncing enthusiasm of a puppy. Pups tend to check out every sniffy smell they come across. Distractions can limit progress on a walk. Don't allow yourself to be pulled in every direction by various distractions. Instead, be more intentional about paying attention to what matters most. You are probably juggling a lot. Everything may feel like a priority, but your success will be limited if you cannot keep all the balls in the air all the time. Consider which of the balls you are juggling are equivalent to glass and must be kept aloft. Which balls are rubber and, if dropped, will bounce back? Being able to distinguish between the two will not only help you retain your sanity but also better prioritize where to focus your time and attention.

TAKE ACTION

1. Maybe you would prefer to spend time figuring out solutions rather than contemplating situations. If reacting to problems is your superpower, are you sure you're working on the right problem? Take time to understand situations. Ask questions to learn more. That friend called "reacting" can turn on you and become an enemy that trips you along the path. Building a discipline of reflection can make you stronger. You'll experience better results and a higher level of energy. Who do you know who is good at picking up on clues that you miss? Seek out their ideas and input and consider these questions:

- What is their secret to noticing things that others overlook?
- How do they prepare for meetings?
- What do they listen for during conversations?
- What do they do that you can adapt to your own personal style?

2. As you refine your noticing abilities, it's important to understand the relationship between holding a leadership role and transforming that leadership into productive action. Otherwise, you can be caught, as Alina and Randall were, in a whirlwind of activity with limited results. Having a leadership title does not, on its own, make you a leader. From time to time, it can

be useful to consider whether your actions reflect the type of leader you aspire to be. The online job site Indeed collected a list of top leadership characteristics that organizations seek. Compare the top leadership characteristics with more negative associations of leaders who may see themselves as "impressive" but are actually ineffective. Which of the qualities on these two lists would your colleagues say best describe you? Which would you most like to develop further?

Top Leadership Characteristics[3]	Anti-Leader Qualities
• Open-minded	• Self-absorbed
• Empathetic	• Poor listener
• Confident	• Smartest person in the room
• Ethical	• Controlling
• Positive	• Loud
• Humble	• Overbearing
• Communicative	• Domineering
• Decisive	• Micromanaging
• Courageous	• Absent (always somewhere more important)
• Accountable	

5.2: BENEFITS OF FLEXIBILITY

Alina and Randall responded differently to the pressure to deliver results while seeking to understand their substantially larger roles. As they brought their tendencies into balance, they were each able to improve their insights and actions. This helped them perform better as their responsibilities expanded. A key aspect for each was the need to connect to their teams and partner with colleagues in a collaborative manner. They wanted to be valued assets, rather than unconsciously vying for approval. In their own way, each desired to be fully in the moment and offer strategic insight. The ability to engage in productive collaborations and reach agreement was important. Leadership flexibility was necessary because they were in rapidly changing work environments. This is true for many in today's organizations. Leaders often have to adapt and move forward without a clear map. Directions relied on in the past are no longer useful.

Victor had always prided himself on quickly assessing situations and knowing what to do next. As his career advanced, he had moved into a senior-level position with a community-based organization. He was discovering that technical knowledge and logic alone were not sufficient to get partners to support his initiatives. It seemed that the more he tried to persuade them to his point of view, the more they dug into their position. He finally admitted to himself that he wasn't getting anywhere and sought out his boss for feedback. That's when an epiphany came in the form of these painful words: "You're really smart, but you don't have all the answers." Victor was working with a number of stakeholders, and when his boss asked what they cared most about, he had to admit he didn't know. Victor could make an educated guess, but how accurate was it? How was he going to reach a workable compromise if he only understood his own bottom line? A certain amount of detachment from his desired outcome was required. Victor wanted to frame his communication with these potential partners in ways they would embrace. To do that, he had to first understand their priorities: what they cared about and where they were willing to compromise. In short, Victor needed to collaborate with others.

This realization was the beginning of Victor's journey to exercise more curiosity and learn—always learn—the *why* behind the *what*. By embracing humility, these skills became invaluable to his career growth and ultimate success. He discovered that the best leaders demonstrate curiosity. While they might have a good idea of where they are going, they remain open to information that could influence a shift in direction.

Leaders sometimes struggle with uncertainty and the ever-changing competitive landscape. Those who conquer the unknowns tend to be more agile in their thinking. They regularly assess the landscape and gather additional insights through alliances and cooperation with others. They are willing to pivot, even when they don't have full information. For leaders in new or evolving situations, this behavior becomes even more important. When you are driving for change, you can bring fresh ideas and approaches to your role. Recognize, however, that changes may have to be made while seeking to understand "the way we've always done it." This is key if you hope to have your team embrace new directions, not just comply with your orders. A client's CEO advised her to "solicit advice before drawing conclusions. Often you may feel you do not need advice but it will facilitate buy-in." That seems straightforward, yet seeking advice when you don't need it is not an automatic action for most people. This is especially true for leaders who are moving toward a goal with confidence.

Even when leaders want to encourage collaboration, they may unintentionally create competition between individuals and teams. Internal win/lose games can have detrimental consequences for the organization and its culture. William P. Barnett of the Stanford Graduate School of Business has studied competition in organizations for decades. He has observed that constant evaluation and comparison among and between team members results in stress and counterproductive behavior.[4] Work to eliminate internal competition. You might focus problem-solving discussions at the organizational, rather than departmental, level. Encourage employees to take appropriate risks. Find a balance between experimentation and results that will be rewarded. It can make a positive difference when mistakes are seen as a chance to learn and improve, individually and as a team. Creating a positive mindset around failures of any kind requires trust. If reliance on others needs a boost, revisit chapter 3 (Trust as a Bridge to Success), share the aspects of trust with your team, and facilitate a discussion.

In addition to agility, a certain level of detachment may be useful, as well, to successfully collaborate. Cultural anthropologist Angeles Arrien observed, "When we find ourselves attached to outcome, our tendency is to control rather than trust. When we are attached to something, we often lose our objectivity about it, and thus lose our ability to do right by it."[5] As a leader, you must identify goals. However, the ability to remain open to fresh thinking will invite your colleagues to help define the path forward. Some adjustments, modifications, and shifts will invariably be required. The information that team members share with you can strengthen your decisions. Tap the wisdom in the room. Those who do typically achieve greater buy-in and more sustainable results.

TAKE ACTION

1. Flexibility and ambiguity are two different things. Vague, uncertain roles, responsibilities, and goals get in the way of team performance. Good collaboration arises from clear goals, well-defined roles, and agreed understanding of responsibilities. These are the "what" aspects of getting things done.

Define these parameters for your team or define them together. Reaching the other side of the lake may be the goal, but there will be more than one way to get there. Allow flexibility in *how* the goal is pursued and trust the team to come up with solutions. That creates greater commitment to the ultimate direction. The team may make some missteps and have to backtrack, so make sure they understand that's okay. Clarity in the beginning and the flexibility that follows can lead to stronger outcomes, greater commitment, and more growth for members of your team.

2. Opportunities for improved flexibility often arise through meetings when curiosity and discussion are regular guests. In his 1980 book, *Cosmos*, astronomer Carl Sagan explained complex scientific ideas about the development of civilization and the world. This observation from the book has stuck with me over the years: "We make our world significant by the courage of our questions and by the depth of our answers." His statement was intended to encourage curiosity about science. It is equally good advice for involving team members in thinking more expansively. Consider how your workplace could be transformed with courageous questions and thoughtful answers that encourage greater adaptability. To move in that direction, here are a few ideas for more productive collaborative conversations:

- Set expectations early in discussions with clear, specific language. For example, saying that you want "active participation" may have a different meaning for you than it does for others. Terms and expected behaviors need to be defined. Remind people of these expectations if the conversation seems to be getting off track.

- Ask specific team members for their thoughts. Instead of general questions such as "What does everyone think?" or "Are there any ideas on this?" ask individuals what they think. Reach out in particular to those who are not already engaged in the discussion.

- If someone is so vocal that they dominate the conversation, appreciate their contributions. Then ask for additional views from others.

- Acknowledge when you are uncertain about a specific direction and invite others' thoughts. Having a strong enough ego to be candid in this way can open the door to stronger connections between colleagues and more powerful team solutions.

A SPECIAL NOTE

It has been said that a truly happy person is one who can enjoy the scenery on a detour. Sometimes, however, detours are stressful and require taking a chance. A certain amount of vulnerability is necessary when using communication skills that enhance trust, collaboration, flexible leadership, and openness to change. This calls for courage. At some point when you exhibit vulnerability, you may take a hit. I have experienced this myself. Don't let yourself get hijacked and react. Can you take the punch? A sense of humor helps. The ability to laugh at yourself (yes, stop taking yourself so seriously) will reduce the impact others can have on you. More tools follow in chapter 6 to help you avoid the "leadership sucks" bus (now leaving from Terminal 2...).

CHECK YOUR GPS

As you travel the road on your leadership journey, be aware of the potential for detours. Distractions can arise in many forms. Of the many demands before you, are you clear on your priorities? How will you remain focused on top priorities while making time to notice what's happening with team members? Observe with curiosity what occurs within your work environment. When you find a way to link your goals and professional interests with those of your colleagues, your potential for collaboration increases. Honing your ability to notice will aid you. Still, at times in every journey, pausing to consider the situation can be useful. Step back to gain a different perspective. Doing so requires slowing down occasionally, the **S** in GPS (Slow Down to Assess and Adjust). Practicing and refining these skills will help you manage the inevitable challenges, disappointments, and detours you encounter along the way.

TRAVEL JOURNAL

As you think about your leadership journey, take a few minutes to consider:

- Do you tend to miss little details or get lost in the weeds? What can you do to move toward balance between the two?

- Where would a pause be most likely to benefit work relationships, your ability to listen and understand, or a collaborative challenge you have encountered?

- What is one thing you could do today to adapt or to clarify priorities? What gets in your way of taking that step?

- Which of these concepts are most relevant to where you are now as a leader?

- How will you use the information in this chapter during the coming week?

CHAPTER 6

When the Obstacle *Is* the Opportunity

"You don't get results by focusing on results. You get results by focusing on the actions that produce results."

— MIKE HAWKINS, PRO FOOTBALL PLAYER

A leader's ability to calmly assess a situation and determine the best course of action is important to professional success. You may need to shift direction because of exciting growth opportunities, or the need for agility could result from negative events outside of your control. Taking a detour is not always the answer. Sometimes obstacles appear and the best choice is to work through them rather than change course. Having tools to chip away at the impediment and clear the path can make all the difference in progress.

In earlier chapters of this book, you learned to open your curiosity and discovered steps to become more self-aware. You then focused on the means to connect with team members and colleagues to build trust. You've identified ways to enhance your leadership presence. These skills allow you to pivot in response to the changing landscape of leadership. As a leader, you have to be agile due to shifts in team membership, organizational changes, and unexpected industry threats and opportunities. It may be lonely at the top but leadership is still an interactive sport. By the very nature of your role, you must engage with others and inspire them to action. Sometimes interpersonal interactions can create communication challenges because of the need to positively influence others. How can you apply the skills in this book to the people issues that occur in your everyday professional life? Obviously, thinking about the desired results doesn't make them magically happen. The actions you take, however, will influence outcomes.

The ability to remain in dialogue, rather than move to persuasion, is key. That means putting aside old-world maps. Those maps won't help you in the rapidly changing world and current role you inhabit. Situations, people, and environments you face may require a different approach to influence positive outcomes. Sometimes there is no choice but to take a detour; however, avoidance is not always an option. The obstacle itself may be the opportunity. Rather than changing course, dealing positively with the challenge—particularly when people are involved—can be where your leadership capabilities shine. This sets you apart. Let's talk about the ability to calmly address conflict and draw out others' ideas. Doing so can help you see over the proverbial horizon to anticipate the opportunities and challenges ahead.

THE BUSINESS CASE FOR CONSTRUCTIVE CONFLICT AND COMMUNICATION

A team of manufacturing leaders wanted to tackle challenges to improve quality and meet their metrics, but had run into issues. They had a new boss, Carla. She was known for her

WHEN THE OBSTACLE *IS* THE OPPORTUNITY

blunt, direct style. At the same time, Carla placed a high value on working well together. The company expected great things with her at the helm, but dissatisfaction and disengagement had increased among the leaders on her team. This was affecting their ability to manage production costs and quality. The result directly affected the organization's bottom line.

It became apparent there was a need for team members to listen to one another and work through issues more productively. For Carla's part, she thought of herself as a great communicator. She enjoyed sharing her point of view and advice with others. It was her way of "giving back," as she put it. After a year in the role, her approach was not working with this group of high performers. Her decisions were being questioned and her team was having trouble resolving issues. Carla was frustrated that her attempts to influence were met, at best, with reluctant compliance. In an effort to have a greater impact, she pushed harder. She held more meetings to share her knowledge and perspective. She did her best to get her team on board with her direction. Carla used her skills of persuasion, but to no avail.

Carla was certain she would make a positive difference for the organization. Her team just needed to listen to her. Discouraged, she was beginning to wonder if they resented her presence. Worse, she suspected some might be hoping she would leave. On interviewing each of the leaders, two issues were revealed. First, conflict was not being managed well. There was also an immediate need to improve information flow. Each leader identified the same problem: everyone else. They were frustrated with Carla and with one another.

Carla placed a high value on getting along. She didn't recognize that the absence of conflict didn't mean there was unity among her leaders. Disagreements had just moved below the surface. Colleagues came to meetings ready to present their ideas but no one was listening to anyone else. When disagreement arose, Carla would intervene. Her idea of conflict management appeared to take one of two approaches: avoidance (e.g., "we'll talk about that later") or command and control (e.g., "I get them in a room together and tell them to cut it out"). In either case, disagreements remained unresolved and collaborative decisions were rarely made. Therein lay the opportunity disguised as an obstacle.

For this Operations group, conflict was not seen as a means to constructively work through issues or get to better solutions. Yet, that is precisely what it can be. Several of the leaders expressed a desire to tackle issues in a more productive manner. But none of them saw their role in the problem. They didn't understand how they were coming across to others. A few team members had developed reputations for being difficult. They tended to react with emotion or ignore data they didn't like. Fortunately, they were interested in working to restore harmony and improve decision-making within the team. They had to get rid of the old maps and chart a new course together based on greater conversational intelligence.

Conversational intelligence requires a different set of communication tools than the team had been using. Collaborative interactions begin with listening. You've already explored the benefits of listening and its connection to trust. (Revisit chapter 2 to refresh your thinking on the superpower of muting yourself. Don't forget the WAIT acronym. Occasionally check in and ask yourself: **W**hy **A**m **I** **T**alking?) Remember to listen to gain information and not just to prepare your reply. When leaders really hear what is being said, great things can happen. Colleagues can open up to possibilities rather than focus on what they'll say next. Working relationships and effectiveness improve.

6.1: HOW DIALOGUE ENHANCES YOUR INFLUENCE

To lead others through the use of influence and inspiration requires sharpening your communication. This is not about beating others into submission or filibustering until they give up and give in. Influence is driven by trust. Think about it. Would you follow someone you don't trust? In chapter 3, you learned that trust is built on dependability, credibility, care, respect, and intention. When the first four elements are present and intentions are clear, you are better able to collaborate with others. You can create stronger solutions and get past the obstacles in your path. William Ury, negotiation guru and author of *Getting to Yes*, has observed that it is possible to face a wide range of challenges when leaders learn to collaborate. He notes that a foundational skill for collaborating is being able to listen with empathy.[1]

You are much more likely to exercise influence when you understand other people—what matters to them and how they can contribute. Here are some steps to help you partner with others, better influence outcomes, and overcome the most daunting obstacles.

Get everyone on the same page. Looking back at the manufacturing leadership team, the competitive landscape had changed. That's one of the reasons Carla was hired. They had evolving marketplace challenges as well as a new boss. Unfortunately, each of them, including Carla, had continued to operate with maps from prior journeys. It was like the team was trying to fly over Dallas using a roadmap of Detroit. Not only were they looking at two different cities but using different modes of transportation. Disconnects like this are not uncommon. Leaders often tend to make decisions based on what has worked for them previously and may focus on what is important to them individually.

> *Recognize that a message sent is not necessarily a message received.*

For a team to operate most effectively, the leader must check assumptions with other members of the team. Without that check-in, inherent bias comes into play. This distorts perspectives and makes it difficult to find alignment. What are the unspoken assumptions? How does each team member define the goal? When everyone on the team is making decisions based on different expectations and conclusions, they end up talking past each other. One fundamental and faulty assumption often made is that everyone interprets information the same way. Recognize that a message sent is not necessarily a message received. Clarify where you are headed and why.

WHEN THE OBSTACLE *IS* THE OPPORTUNITY

Move into dialogue. Once the goal has been clearly stated, conversation about how to get there comes next. There are many paths to the top of the mountain. Your preferred path as the leader carries weight, but others might know a shortcut, a safer route, or one that is more scenic. Each way has potential value. When there is more than one person involved, there will likely be multiple interpretations.

If you engage solely in advocacy for your perspective, you may miss something important. Recognize when you are in "sell" mode. Persuasion is not dialogue. Yes, sometimes a leader has to tell team members how the cow ate the cabbage. If you're unfamiliar with this colloquialism, it's a memorable way of saying that the leader is telling it like it is. Sometimes leaders have to take a hard line and expect everyone to get on board. This is easier when there is a trusting relationship—another reason why trust is foundational for successful leaders.

The team may not agree. They may want to execute a different plan. More importantly, they may know something you do not that would make a difference in the plan. When you are the leader, how do you find out? Stop giving directions for a moment and recognize that you are at a crossroads. This is an opportunity to invite dialogue. Let go of your preferred outcome (or the one you insist upon) just for a moment, and listen with curiosity and empathy.

Carla practiced "tell-sell-yell" behavior. She was highly directive (tell), her go-to approach was persuasion (sell), and she wasn't above ripping into a team member if she was stressed or facing a deadline (yell). She was certain how the manufacturing team should move forward. If only they would listen, they would see things her way. Unfortunately, pushing her agenda harder made her team dig in their heels. They didn't feel heard or respected and they questioned her motives. As a result, trust was reduced. Carla needed to repair trust by engaging her team of high-performing leaders in a different way.

Unlike Carla's initial approach, dialogue is something done *with* others. It is not something done *to* them. Moving away from directive behavior required a shift in attitude. Carla had to let go of the desire to be right. She needed to create space for her team members to engage with her in diagnosing and solving problems. Everyone thought they had *the* answer and no one was listening to anyone else. Changing this way of interacting required a change in behavior at the top. Though everyone in the room had to control their desire to make the winning argument, Carla was the executive in charge. It was her job to model desired behavior and hold others accountable to follow. The goal was to gain agreement on a path forward. With a shared position, they could then advance toward a more open exploration of possibilities. Note that this change was not about gaining consensus. Sometimes there will be disagreement (more on that in the next section). Still, engaging in curious and open dialogue allowed team members to express their ideas. The team began to create something together which helped move them to better solutions.

Share your perspective and draw out others. Remember the observation in chapter 4 that once a leader speaks, exploration and inquiry tend to stop? When you focus on persuasion, team members will typically move into execution mode. They begin thinking about how to bring your idea to life. You may feel compelled to put your solution on the table. Don't simply advocate your perspective, though. If you feel it is necessary to state your position, explain how you arrived at that solution. You might say that you developed your idea based on the information available and are wondering how to make it better. Invite your audience to find ways to improve your solution.

Purposefully pause to check in with the team. This may require periodically inviting each person to say something. Be sure to listen without comment or defense; you are in information-gathering mode. Inviting active participation has the added advantage of creating a more inclusive environment. Each team member can say "no comment," but everyone has to say something. While it can take time for everyone on the team to be comfortable with this approach, as this becomes a regular practice, they will be more engaged. Mutual exchange of information and dialogue is more likely to happen. As you encourage and model success with this approach, urge them to use the technique with their own teams as well.

Exercise influence. Influence is not about winning the day with the most persuasive argument. It's engaging others to join you in addressing a common goal or challenge. It is difficult to influence without a relationship. While leaders exercise a certain amount of position power, they tend to get compliance, not adoption, if they push their own agenda. Asking curious, open-ended questions and listening to the replies gives space for a relationship to develop. Really ... stop talking and listen. As new information comes to light, look for patterns in the complexity of situations and think several moves ahead. Rather than binary yes/no or good/bad judgments and win/lose games, consider intermediate positions. How can you incorporate ideas to engage more people in pursuing a new direction? It is possible to be influential without getting everything you want. Influence is about incorporating your position with others' objectives rather than resisting their objections.

Perhaps you have thought of influence skills as belonging to the verbally gifted, those silver-tongued persuaders who could convince anyone of anything. In reality, your influence as a leader is enhanced by hearing others' stories. Acknowledging different points of view creates a connection. Being open to new ways of thinking invites similar behavior from colleagues. These are all dialogue skills that can be developed with intentionality and practice. They can increase your influence because this ability inextricably intertwines with your connections to others.

> *When you are able to influence others, your voice is more likely to be heard and your contributions acknowledged.*

Your capacity to guide people through change and uncertainty matters. Your team's trust that you have their individual—and the organization's—best interests at heart makes a difference. These skills represent your ability to gain support, even from those who have a different point of view. Your open, curious manner takes the pressure off them to

WHEN THE OBSTACLE *IS* THE OPPORTUNITY

agree with you. It gives them an opportunity to change their thinking, attitude, or behavior. When you are able to influence others, your voice is more likely to be heard and your contributions acknowledged on a broader scale.

TAKE ACTION

1. Interactions based on trust tend to advance collaboration and teamwork. If you seek to improve communication within and across teams, take a good, hard, honest look at actions that negatively impact trust. If there is blame, replace it with curiosity. This week, think like a chess player or maybe a rock climber (whichever appeals more). Both contemplate several moves ahead. When your leadership journey has taken you into the wilderness, this analogy may be more useful than you think.

Ask yourself: If this happens, then what will we do? How can I prepare now? Considering the implications, consequences, and contingencies of your decisions helps you anticipate reactions and plan countermoves. At the same time, the goal is not to outmaneuver others. Sincerely think through your actions and choices. What are the truly unexpected results that could occur? If they do, how can you remain open to additional information? Doing so will help you continue moving through the obstacle or determine if a pivot is needed.

2. If your goal is to move beyond superficial, polite conversation, engage in more authentic interactions. Doing so creates opportunity to discover additional information. While your ideas may be superb, if they are only yours, they likely will not result in

sustainable change. Move away from short-term wins and pursue transformation that truly takes root. When you are successful at inviting a broader audience to be part of the conversation and the solution, you can create an environment where continuous improvement flourishes. This can lead to change that will more successfully gain traction. Consider these strategies:

- Approach conversations as an opportunity to partner with others, not convince them of your solution. What meaning can they add to the discussion?

- Consider the context of comments. As you listen to input and discussion, think before responding. Keep overall objectives in mind.

- Pay attention to nonverbal indicators. As you listen to what is being said, how do voice tone and body language reflect others' thoughts? What can you learn that helps you appeal to their interest in the group's overarching goals?

- Act as a partner. This requires respecting opinions and letting go of the assumption that you have all the answers. There may be something you need to know that you aren't aware of yet. How can you discover that information?

- Engage in a balance of advocacy for your position and inquiry to understand other perspectives. Are you looking for compliance or the best solution? Ask questions to understand what assumptions others are making. Don't compound the problem by making your own assumptions. Seek clarity.

6.2: CONFLICT IS NOT A DIRTY WORD

Conflict can arise from efforts to engage team members in collaboration. Even though the result of conflict may be productive, leaders often inadvertently push disagreement below the surface. This happens when they express a desire for everyone to get along or work well together above all else. Such discomfort with conflict can result in passive-aggressive behavior. Team members try to follow directives to be agreeable and lack the skill to productively address disagreements. Conflict may appear to be absent but lack of resolution causes aggressive behaviors to occur outside of the leader's view. Better results come when leaders model constructive dissent. They actively invite different perspectives and hold team members accountable to talk things out. The challenge for most leaders is learning how to work through the conflicts that inevitably arise. Here are some ideas for how to walk a different path.

Like an unattended blister on a long hike, a difficult conversation doesn't get better—or easier—with time. It usually gets worse. Even when you know that, you might avoid having the difficult conversation out of fear of conflict. Why is it that conflict is uncomfortable for so many? Is it a desire to please? Or maybe their mom, like my own, said, "If you can't say something nice, don't say anything at all." It could be that some leaders lack the patience to work through the messiness of conflict. If they already have an idea of how they want to proceed, they may not see any benefit in addressing disputed points. Whatever the cause, most leaders tend to avoid behavior that will be perceived as argumentative. They associate happy, productive teams with a lack of conflict. Yet good communicators aren't afraid of disagreement. They respond with curiosity rather than defensiveness. They see pushback as a way to build better outcomes.

Let's frame conflict as bringing different perspectives to the surface. The goal is to respond thoughtfully and say, "I see things differently." By avoiding reactive, emotional responses, you can encourage healthy debate. You can nurture alternative points of view for constructive dissent. It is worth noting that conflict management is not the same as crisis management. Being good at fighting fires does not mean that disagreements are being productively addressed.

One way of thinking about conflict is based on a model created by Kenneth W. Thomas and Ralph H. Kilmann. It compares the extent to which each person attempts to satisfy their own concerns versus how much they seek to meet others' concerns. The model identifies five approaches for responding to conflict. Each approach compares a person's focus on their own concerns (measured as level of assertiveness) in relation to others' concerns (measured as level of cooperativeness).[2] It is easy to get stuck when one method is overused. When that happens, you tend not to move through conflict situations in a productive manner. The five approaches identified in the Thomas-Kilmann Conflict Mode

WHEN THE OBSTACLE *IS* THE OPPORTUNITY

Instrument (TKI) are: competing, accommodating, avoiding, collaborating, and compromising. It takes skill, self-awareness, and honesty to recognize where you operate most of the time. This is where you are most comfortable and where you are likely to go when under stress. Once you recognize the style you use most frequently, you can adjust for a given situation as you pursue a better outcome. Each of the approaches can be appropriate in certain situations, though the goal is to reach compromise, a balance of assertiveness and cooperation.

> *Competing* represents those who are high on assertiveness and low on cooperation. This is a comfortable place for leaders who have been successful and who are used to winning. You can overdo it, though, when everything becomes a contest and you feel a relentless need to be right all the time.
>
> *Accommodating* embodies those who are high on cooperation and low on assertiveness. Leaders tend to use this approach when it is most important to protect the relationship. For example, you may prefer a different outcome, but agree to support the group decision to preserve harmony.
>
> *Avoiding* is a style that is low on both assertiveness and cooperation. This represents a level of disengagement that could signal several things. You may be indifferent or believe the issue is not important. Or, you might be sidestepping the conflict to allow temperatures to cool—though it is important that issues put off until later are still addressed.

Collaborating is characterized by those high on both assertiveness and cooperation. Those skilled at collaborating will often look for common purpose. They are essentially seeking a win/win solution. They may get creative to find an answer that satisfies all parties.

Compromising represents the middle of the road on both. Compromisers tend to view others as negotiating partners. They are realistic about what can be achieved. When compromising, you recognize that sometimes each side has to give a little to reach a satisfactory solution.

The TKI is useful beyond thinking about conflict. A willingness to cooperate is often based on trust. For any communication situation, consider how you interact with others. If you feel yourself pulled away from cooperation, it may be useful to revisit the foundational components of trust in that relationship (chapter 3). When trust is present, you are more comfortable balancing your personal perspective with those of others. Then it is easier to move away from persuasion and toward more productive dialogue.

In addition, take responsibility for your own thoughts and actions during conflict situations. In chapter 4, steps to identify when you have been triggered were outlined. Rather than reacting, you can get better results when you are able to recognize your response and be more thoughtful in how you reply. Good leaders own their contributions to situations that have gone awry. You may feel you have done everything right. This is not about taking all the blame for a bad result.

WHEN THE OBSTACLE *IS* THE OPPORTUNITY

Leaders are more effective when they recognize how they contributed to a situation that didn't go well, even if their part was only one percent of the poor outcome. Considering how you balance cooperation and assertiveness may help identify what you can do differently.

Carla had to take responsibility so that she could get beyond her earlier, failed efforts. She wanted to build better connections with her team. Each team member had to let go of their desire to score individual points and instead become more cooperative. As they opened up to hearing additional views, they were able to increase their comfort with constructive conflict. In this group of high performers, winning whatever competition came along was highly prized. Everyone loves a winner, but they had lost sight of where the real competition properly resided. It was in the marketplace, not with each other. Most people are hardwired to hate losing even more than they love to win. When you are not competing with your colleague, though, you won't feel a need to outdo that person. You can work together to find the best solution. In Carla's case, because she had prioritized getting along, conflict had gone underground. Her leadership team members were pretending to agree, but they were still in competitive mode. Their disagreements weren't being addressed. The conflict began coming out in unproductive behaviors that undermined the entire organization.

Helping Carla and her team avoid win/lose games was important. They had to slow down, recognize their impulse to win at all costs, and be willing to identify mutual goals. What was in the best interests of the company? They needed to care equally about results *and* their relationships with one another. Then they could take advantage of the collective brilliance of the team. This didn't happen overnight. Once they were able to do it successfully, though, their metrics improved. The manufacturing team once again delivered strong performance.

TAKE ACTION

1. Stephen R. Covey famously said, "Seek first to understand. Then be understood," the fifth habit in Covey's *7 Habits* book. This observation is unlike the manufacturing leaders who wanted to be heard first before anyone else spoke. They were not seeking to understand. In their case, it was about getting credit for having the right answer. They wanted to prove their wisdom and value. It was almost as if they were afraid to hear what others might suggest. Wait, you may be saying, is this about listening? Again?! That's right. What do you *not* know? If you turn on your curiosity and really listen, you might be surprised by what you discover.

Egos can get in the way of even the best-functioning teams. Conflict is natural when driven, successful people are passionate about their ideas. When disagreement is handled well, your team can achieve better results. Here are a few suggestions:

- Watch for goals that have become "mine" instead of "ours." When that happens, team members may not be helping each other to succeed.

- Silos—business divisions and departments that avoid sharing information—are dangerous. Take an attitude of service to help your colleagues over time. This can result in reciprocal support and break down silos.

- One of the most effective ways to stop team members from complaining about others is to force direct communication with one another. In other words, when a team member comes to you with an issue involving a colleague, a meeting with both people is in order. Don't allow triangulation. Call the other person in and speak with both of them together, or have the person who brought the issue to your attention talk directly with their coworker. Ask that both follow up with you, together. Allowing separate conversations may feel like keeping the peace, but conflict avoidance does nothing to resolve issues.

- Respect is a key element. Understand that everyone is trying to do their best. Just because you disagree doesn't mean the other person is wrong. There is a simplistic way to think of differences of opinion: Whether a printed number looks like a **6** or a **9** depends on which direction you see the number from. Perspective matters.

- Stay focused on the big picture. If another person or group is struggling, rather than getting angry, ask how you can help. If you or your group are struggling, don't be defensive. Be supportive of what others need and help each other reduce roadblocks.

2. *Nemawashi* is the Japanese word for road-testing and strengthening ideas. While this practice can lay the foundation for acceptance of a proposal, the concept is also about building relationships and communicating clearly. The intention is to create allies. As feedback is gathered, you modify your proposal and continue to gather support. The ultimate goal is to move toward consensus. The process of *nemawashi* recognizes that some ideas simply won't be successful, and that's okay. It invites dissent without disagreement. By talking to people in decision-making roles, you gather input and your ideas evolve. Incorporating suggestions also increases the likelihood of broader support. These actions can lead to better decisions and may ultimately be very different from where you started.[3]

CHECK YOUR GPS

Increasing your comfort with disagreement is one example of how to apply the **S** (Slow Down to Assess and Adjust) in GPS. Clearly state your expectations and listen to alternative perspectives. This will enhance your influence and perceived effectiveness as a leader. Healthy dialogue and robust collaboration contribute to constructive conflict management. Recognize that conflict happens. Help team members move beyond the view that disagreement is about individual personalities. Leaders who use their talents to invite insight and listen carefully will find that they are seen as stronger communicators. They can enhance dialogue through their own interactions. Their emphasis on how differences of opinion lead to stronger outcomes also benefits the team. Above all, if you remain flexible and open to various perspectives, stay curious, and listen, you'll have the ability to draw greater intelligence from the team. These skills will help you tackle obstacles in your path with improved results.

Malcolm X, a well-known and vocal spokesperson for the Nation of Islam, was a controversial figure. He was quite comfortable clearly stating his path in ways that were often argumentative and sometimes led to violence. Many people still think of him in this way. Yet his views evolved over time and eventually he distanced himself from prior associations. It's been said that Malcolm X observed, "When 'I' is replaced by 'we,' even illness becomes wellness." Though not interested in collaboration or dialogue when he first rose to prominence, he came to see the value of working together. Moving away from "my" view to a broader perspective can benefit everyone. Ultimately, the actions that lead to better results are worth your time and attention.

TRAVEL JOURNAL

As you think about your leadership journey, take a few minutes to consider:

- Where are you more focused on results than relationships right now? What is one thing you could do to move toward balance between the two?

COURAGEOUS CLARITY

- What type of competitive behaviors (aka "winning") get in the way of productive dialogue on your team?
- Where do you feel most stuck?
- Which of these concepts are most relevant to where you are now as a leader?
- How will you use the information in this chapter in the next meeting you attend?

CHAPTER 7

It's Not All Smooth Sailing

"The problem with being a person of integrity is that it can put you at a disadvantage when dealing with people who aren't. They have more options."

— DR. STANLEY J. WARD, LEADERSHIP COACH

"There is a lot that is good about leadership but…" After focusing on the many right things you can do as a leader, it is important to acknowledge that leadership is not always a pleasant journey. You may execute perfectly, yet there are still things you can't control. No formula guarantees success. Even in the best organizations, there will be rough patches. The longer you are under stress, the harder it is to use your soft skills well as emotions run high. If you feel swept overboard, coming up for air is important. Become the kind of person who can handle both success and failure. Sometimes things just don't work out. When you fail, don't neglect self-care. Allow time for restorative activities. Build your resilience. Then rise again to take on new challenges with renewed vigor.

Leaders can develop and increase their ability to anticipate and respond to detours and obstacles, whether expected or not. While the tools provided in this book will make you a better, more effective leader, minefields lurk below the surface in most organizations. Occasionally there are storms that require you to batten down the hatches. Acknowledge these hazards and learn to address them.

Every organization operates in its own way with a different set of rules or political interaction. While you may seek to do your work with integrity, being conscious of how others "play the game" can equip you for situations that might otherwise create a hazard. What follows is hardly a comprehensive list of potential pitfalls. It *is* an assessment of four common issues faced by organizational leaders.

- Assuming that "doing the right thing" will be rewarded in the organization;

- Focusing on results to the exclusion of relationships;

- Stepping on someone else's turf, usually inadvertently and with good intentions; and

- Assuming trust where none has been built.

Every organization has some level of political interaction. Without an understanding of the political environment in your organization, your best intentions may be misguided. Those who refuse to play politics doom themselves. There is value in positive politics. Such interactions should address the allocation of resources in a productive manner. If you want to be effective in your role, it is important to understand where political whirlpools exist. They are there, in every organization. Collaboration and constructive conflict help to address these challenges to a certain extent, but won't eliminate pitfalls from your work life. Still, these skills provide a good starting point and foundation to address challenges. Where there are people, there are politics. As you strengthen your understanding of your work environment, you will be better able to take on the unexpected.

7.1: ASSUMING THAT "DOING THE RIGHT THING" WILL BE REWARDED

Most leaders assume that their organizations are reputable and ethical, and that "doing the right thing" will be rewarded. That isn't always the case. Sometimes those with ulterior motives seem to reap the greatest rewards. If you are not paying attention, you may find yourself in a political quagmire.

John's career was taking off when he joined a technology company that others saw as driving innovative change. He looked forward, in particular, to partnering with his new colleague Andy, a legend in the industry. Together, he saw ways they could advance the organization. John quickly learned, however, that Andy had made himself invaluable to the CEO by sharing information and stroking the CEO's ego, not through technological brilliance. His success and "legendary" status were built on questionable practices.

Andy understood what the CEO cared most about and delivered, time and again. He was less well loved by his colleagues because he often told them one thing and the CEO something else. Andy had razor-sharp focus on elevating himself. Even those who attempted to work collegially with him, like John, found that information they shared was often used against them. Andy seemed to thrive on encouraging a *Hunger Games* battle-to-the-death approach to work. He sought to advance his career and elevate his personal status, frustrating those around him. When Andy eventually fell from grace, no one was surprised. John certainly was not disappointed to see him go.

Most leaders have known an Andy at some point in their careers. They likely referred to that person as being "political." A survey of senior leaders produced a number of comments about organizational politics. Definitions covered a range of responses, visceral and mostly negative, including:

- Working a personal agenda;

- Putting up obstacles because you don't want to change;

- Protecting turf;

- Two (or more) groups with different views and opinions who don't want to listen to one another or work together;

- Making decisions based on individual feelings or connections rather than business need;

- Lobbying a position that best suits your needs versus what is in the best interests of a project;

- Informally presenting an idea in an attempt to gain favor; and

- Acting to receive attention or accolades regardless of whether it benefits the company.

IT'S NOT ALL SMOOTH SAILING

As evidenced by this list, many leaders have negative associations with the term "organizational politics." The practice of politics within companies is often perceived as the domain of colleagues more interested in currying favor than accomplishing tasks. Those said to be playing politics are considered disingenuous and of suspect motive, lowering trust.

In spite of these perceptions, some level of political competency is necessary for leaders to succeed. Politics need not be toxic and there is a cost if you don't engage. Disengaging can allow those with less knowledge and experience to drive decision-making. Refusing to participate can disadvantage you and your team. Instead, choose how you will play. Rather than checking out, consider viewing corporate politics through a different lens. Resources are scarce within organizations. Allocation of those scarce resources is driven by political decision-making: outcomes influenced by relationships, connections, limited information, and individual dreams and ambitions. This is neither good nor bad. It just is. You can take part in a professional way and maintain your integrity. First, you must recognize the power structure and currency of exchange in your organization.

There are many types of power in organizations.[1] Generally, power flows from either the position an individual holds or how they interact with others. People might be seen as powerful because of title and responsibilities. By virtue of their position, leaders are able to bestow rewards on others—itself a form of power. Leaders may compel compliance through fear of punishment if others don't follow their directions. Perhaps someone has access to information that others do not. Knowledge really is power. Information access can provide that person with the ability to enlighten others or use what they know as a bargaining chip. Each of these sources of power is typically associated with position. While potent, such power can be heady but often fleeting.

Relying too heavily on position power may have short-term advantages. At the same time, it can weaken relationships and cause resentment. More constructive power comes from attributes such as colleagues respecting, and feeling respected by, you. This is known as referent power. Combined with your knowledge, skills, and experience, the relationships you develop in an organization can give you a foundation for influence. That influence can be powerful.

Power alone, however, is typically not sufficient. A helpful starting place may be to distinguish between what the recruiting literature for the organization says and what actually gets rewarded. What matters to others in your workplace?[2] Answering that question will help you understand if "doing the right thing" will be enough to succeed. Just as there are many forms of power, there are many forms of currency. If your only sense of self-worth is based on how well you are paid or the position you hold, you will tend not to invest in relational currency.

In Andy's story, he made presumptions about where to invest in relationships. He ignored the opportunity to create allies and advocates within the organization. Anyone can be a potential ally. They are the colleagues who run alongside you, pursuing the same vision. Advocates are those who take additional steps and invest in your success in some way, even if it is simply telling others about the value of your work. It is good to have one or the other. Over time, you ideally develop both.

By ignoring the value of positive relationships, Andy perpetuated toxic behavior that negatively impacted the team. For him, at least in the short term, his poor behavior was rewarded. Doing the right thing doesn't always produce the desired results.

Recognize that every organization has a primary currency through which power is held and results achieved. Understanding this doesn't mean that the Andys of the world will automatically be defeated, but awareness can help you identify potential minefields. As you gain insight into the currency of the organization, that knowledge can help you navigate the turbulence of political currents. Even if you choose to behave differently, you should be able to work more productively with colleagues because you will understand what they value.

NAVIGATING THIS MINEFIELD: ORGANIZATIONAL POLITICS

Anyone can be a potential ally. However, this does not mean we should use each other to reach our goals. It is healthiest to let go of a mindset that says, "Do unto others *before* they do unto you." This type of thinking causes you to engage in constant threat-seeking. By default, you are then likely to interpret every situation through a negative lens. At the same time, be aware that some of your colleagues may trade primarily on the currencies of position power. Connection and collaborative relationships may take a back seat. So how do you remain true to your desire to be a positive, productive leader when others around you don't care how many bodies they leave behind?

Here are some things to consider:

- Seek to understand what matters most to those challenging colleagues. This requires curiosity and listening (chapter 2). Don't confuse curiosity with interrogation. The point is not to ask question after question after question, but to be open to different views, seek to learn more, and truly listen.

- Also be aware of how your interactions are or are not building trust (chapter 3). Look for ways to help others succeed. This can advance everyone's interests. It is pragmatism, not manipulation.

- At the same time, beware of the lure of wins that force you to compromise your values. For example, someone may prize put-downs and see them as joking around. You see the damage that does to relationships and trust, but need to work together more amicably with this person. How can you resist the urge to give in to get along? Your behavior can serve as an influence for a different way of doing business. You may not directly challenge their abuse, but you don't have to join in with mean-spirited banter.

- Depending on the level of vitriol, it may be best to focus your efforts elsewhere while still being mindful of the games that the Andys of the organization play.

IT'S NOT ALL SMOOTH SAILING

Few people intentionally want to be "that guy" (Andy) who is so blatantly and toxically political. At the opposite end of the spectrum is Barbara. She found herself in a new leadership role where team members were masterful at playing the game. It would have been easy to go to battle over political gamesmanship, but Barbara was a seasoned corporate leader and had a good instinct for how to diffuse unproductive behavior.

Rather than come in like a bulldozer, ready to push back with sweeping change, Barbara focused on getting to know her colleagues. She sought to understand what was most important to them and looked for ways to help them succeed. Self-interest is a very real thing. Barbara knew it could be helpful to appeal to self-interest when dealing with political behavior. She wasn't interested in creating an adversarial relationship between her perspective and theirs. Instead, she got curious about how and why they had come to practice political maneuvering as a fine art. Through her interactions, she was able to determine which team members might be open to a different way of working together.

Sometimes the only way forward is to face the headwinds. This is essentially what it means for a sailboat to tack from side to side. A sailboat captain changes course and heads into the wind. Similarly, Barbara thought about how to work with existing politics instead of fight against them. She identified how the organization rewarded those who played politics. She listened, without blame or judgment, to understand who the key decision makers were and what they cared most about. Then she thought about how this information could be put to better use for the benefit of the entire team. As Barbara built trust, she was also able to position herself as an influencer, ready to move the team toward collaboration. Often influence works like this. While you may be tempted to actively persuade someone to behave differently, that can feel to them more like manipulation. Greater success can come through understanding others' perspectives and appealing to their self-interests. While you can't control the wind, you can always adjust your rudder and your sails.

Experience supports Barbara's successful approach. She thoughtfully studied the currencies of power. This allowed her to understand what the organization valued and how she could influence a shift away from power-driven behavior. Trying to sell her perspective would have been a battle. Instead, she spoke to decision makers' self-interests in order to win their support. This is similar to the way that salespeople interested in long-term relationships with their customers look for ways to build value for the client. Barbara wouldn't have characterized her approach as sales, but she focused less on changing minds and more on developing trusting relationships and adding value. Over time she was quite successful in her efforts.

7.2: FOCUSING ON RESULTS TO THE EXCLUSION OF RELATIONSHIP: A COROLLARY TO INSIGHTS ON POWER AND POLITICAL CURRENCY

A recognized "high-potential" leader, Scott's career was on an upward trajectory when he accepted a senior director role in a new department. He had heard that his new boss, Rhonda, could be challenging, but Scott was self-confident. His past ability to overcome issues through stellar performance caused him to brush aside this information. Six months into the job, however, Scott felt that Rhonda was questioning the quality of his work and his colleagues were working to undermine him. This had never happened before. Scott was concerned that he was being set up to fail.

In conversations outside of their department, Scott painted a picture of Rhonda that was less than flattering. He was sure she was in over her head. He felt she didn't know how to deal with other team members who were threatened by Scott's success. This may have been true, but in any organization, finding a way to work productively with your boss and colleagues is a necessary skill set. Scott needed to explore and unpack what he might do differently. Though frustrated, he decided he needed to improve trust and develop better working relationships.

Fairly quickly, it became clear that Scott had defined himself in terms of title and earnings. He measured himself relative to others in that way. It wasn't that he flaunted his salary or how quickly he had risen in the company, even though he was proud of his accomplishments. Besides, he didn't need to say anything. Others regularly commented on his rapid rise. Instead, he made decisions as to where he would spend his time and energy based on what had always worked for him in the past. All that mattered was to deliver over and above expectations.

What Scott missed with this approach, however, was that his achievements were fleeting. Over the long term, his behavior negatively impacted how he was perceived. This is the classic Pyrrhic victory, named for the Greek king who fought the Romans and won several decisive victories, yet incurred so many casualties that morale fell and he was ultimately defeated. All leaders need the support of the people around them to be successful and Scott was no exception. He worked for a relationship-driven executive. Rhonda had been in her role for eight years and had built a successful team. They were collaborative, even though they each had separate areas of responsibility. She was challenging, yes, and also fair.

Scott was investing more time and effort in his work than in getting to know his new boss or his colleagues—with whom he felt he had little or no common responsibilities. He didn't understand their perspectives and challenges. He'd shown more commitment to his own success than to theirs. Scott was essentially defining himself as a team of one. He lacked the vision for how the entire department could support the organization. As a result, his colleagues had concluded that Scott was in it only for himself. They didn't want him on the team and were bringing concerns to Rhonda on a regular basis. Scott's suspicions were right. They were working against him.

IT'S NOT ALL SMOOTH SAILING

Focusing on results to the exclusion of everything else caused Scott to ignore actions he could have taken. It was in his control to smooth his acceptance into the group. That also would have made him a more valuable contributor to the organization as a whole.

Fortunately for Scott, his desire to get back on track helped him accept his contribution to the problem. By stepping off the path and pausing for a moment, he recognized what he needed to do differently. Scott began to work on self-reflection, approaching co-workers with curiosity (and applying many of the Take Action exercises outlined in earlier chapters). This slowed down his decision-making, which felt antithetical to getting results. While it was hard for Scott to change habits that had catapulted him to success, it ultimately worked. His persistence and commitment to addressing the issue repaired connections. Those relationships contributed to his success while in the senior director role and long after he left that department.

NAVIGATING THIS MINEFIELD: INTERPERSONAL DYNAMICS

Understanding formal and informal power dynamics in organizations—learning "who's who in the zoo"—is challenging enough. Beyond the formal org chart, it is helpful to pay attention to interpersonal dynamics. Organizational psychologist and author Adam Grant[3] has identified those in organizations who, like Scott, tend to be in it for themselves. Grant calls these negative cultural influencers Takers. Further along the continuum are leaders who engage in quid pro quo behavior (i.e., you take care of me and I'll take care of you). Grant refers to these people as Matchers. They are often the most successful in the workplace. At the opposite end of the spectrum are Givers. Givers are people who go above and beyond for others. Interestingly, Grant found that Givers tend not to be the strongest performers. This may be because they are too busy helping everyone else. From a macro perspective, however, organizations that have more Givers than Takers tend to have better overall outcomes. While adding more Givers and Matchers to your organization doesn't necessarily change results, getting rid of Takers is essential. As with the Pyrrhic victory, succeeding as a Taker may feel good for a while, until you lose your job.

Though Scott was demonstrating Taker tendencies, he was not unusual among high-potential leaders, and for good reason. Organizations value and reward results. The consulting firm Zenger Folkman surveyed 95,000 managers about the skills most important to success.[4] Responses suggest that those who are more results-driven tend to be more highly valued in organizations. However, the study's findings don't end there. Leaders who are able to balance the pursuit of results with nurturing of relationships are even more highly prized. This is true, at least in part, because those leaders are so rare.

How do you balance drive for results with connection to colleagues? Do you approach work relationships as a Giver, Taker, or Matcher? Now may be a good time to pause and consider what you can do differently. A shift may be in order. Consider what behavior your boss expects from you. Just as importantly, what do you expect of yourself? At a minimum, understand that helping others succeed can help you too.

7.3: STEPPING ON ANOTHER'S TURF (INTENTIONALLY OR INADVERTENTLY)

Sometimes even the best intentions can go sideways. Santiago was hired by a fast-growing startup because of his experience in Fortune 100 companies. He brought to the company a strong sense of leadership and drive to get things done. His new boss expressed expectations that Santiago would "upscale" the department. The company looked to him to implement processes that would evolve as the company grew. He was excited about the possibilities.

Within a few months of his arrival, a colleague asked Santiago what was wrong with his team. "What do you mean?" he asked, puzzled. One team member had just resigned (but did not tell Santiago). The others were complaining to anyone who would listen. They said he was making changes without understanding why they did things the way they did. They claimed he reassigned work before determining who had what expertise, and was inserting himself into situations where he was not needed. Santiago called a team meeting. He stated that he wanted to hear their concerns directly, not via colleagues on the senior leadership team. Then he stopped talking and waited for someone to speak.

Several of them acted like they didn't know what Santiago was talking about. Then one manager offered a hesitant observation. She said that Santiago had changed a project plan before they had an opportunity to review it with him. He asked a few clarifying questions and thanked the manager for speaking up. Another jumped in to say that their previous boss had not been involved in projects to the extent that Santiago was. This team member expressed frustration at being micromanaged and questioned why he didn't trust them. The discussion unwound from there. It was a difficult conversation. Santiago realized as he listened to their comments that he had assumed they knew why he was making changes. He had focused on getting to work, rather than sitting down to share his tasks with the team and strategizing together on ways to move forward. They felt their turf had been invaded and were building reinforcements to battle—and possibly reject—the newcomer.

NAVIGATING THIS MINEFIELD: COMMUNICATION AND ROLE CLARITY

In the absence of information, as discussed before, people will draw conclusions based on past experience. Such behavior is amplified when team members don't understand your intentions. Perhaps they feel threatened. Maybe they had someone act in a similar way and are reacting to history that you know nothing about. Don't assume that they will be as excited about change as you are. It will likely bother those who have more ownership or attachment to the way things are currently done. It is also important to acknowledge that sometimes team members didn't get the memo (or any communication) indicating the scope of your new role. You may assume you are in charge of a project but that isn't as clear to colleagues.

Role clarity can help. Determining who is responsible for what can influence how effectively teams work together. Communicating that information before a project proceeds can reduce misunderstandings and increase clarity. A tool for greater transparency around roles and responsibilities is RACI. This model gives team members a common language to discuss expectations and reach agreement.

RACI stands for Responsible, Accountable, Consulted, and Informed. The **R** in RACI is the person or group who owns an initiative, project, or task. They get the work done. The **A** represents the group or individuals to whom the *responsible* person is *accountable*. The person or persons designated as accountable are the ultimate decision makers.

For most initiatives, there will be people who need to be *consulted* before a decision is made because they have information that will be useful to the project. Their role is to provide the best information possible, similar to a second opinion you might seek from a physician. The leader in a **C** role knows that she is not the decision maker, nor is she responsible to make things happen. Her role is to contribute insight and expertise needed to make a well-informed choice. When someone is *informed* under the RACI model, they are brought into the loop once a decision has been made or action taken because it impacts their work. The person in an **I** role knows that he is not the decision maker and does not have any input into the outcome because the direction has already been set.

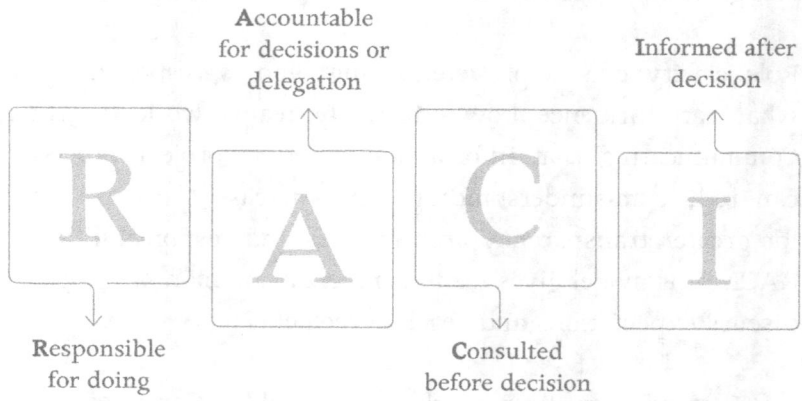

A leadership team I worked with used RACI to improve communication between members simply by incorporating references to "consult" and "inform" in their interactions. A brief discussion helped to prevent misunderstandings when everyone had the same understanding of what those words meant. Determining that people (or positions) fell into the C or I role and communicating that to the current person in that role before a project proceeded reduced misunderstandings and improved communication. Previously, one leader might have asked another for their ideas. If suggestions weren't adopted, the leader who was asked to share their expertise would be insulted that their feedback was ignored. By saying, "I want to consult you on this issue," colleagues understood what they were being asked to do. There is more information about RACI in the endnotes for this chapter if you are interested in a framework that might help your organization improve in this area.[5]

IT'S NOT ALL SMOOTH SAILING

This framework is not just about clarifying who is doing what. There is value in having common terminology and ensuring an open conversation takes place about what team members need from one another. If someone is consulted and thinks they should be responsible for the ultimate decision, it brings to the surface a necessary discussion that helps prevent power struggles and team members working at cross-purposes. RACI is a useful model to facilitate conversations that enhance understanding across all parties.

Beyond role clarity, good communication can go a long way toward avoiding turf wars. This might include asking for input and ideas, validating others' perspectives, and clearly stating your intentions. Refresh your practices of listening and perspective-taking (chapter 2) to help with this challenge.

7.4: ASSUMING TRUST WHERE NONE HAS BEEN BUILT

To create stronger connections with his C-level colleagues, Ed reached out to Greg to discuss a proposal. Ed wanted to improve financial controls within the organization. As a new CFO, he saw great opportunity to upgrade these processes. He also worried that some requests coming from a particular Board member could result in actions that might be seen as questionable by federal regulators.

Greg had been General Counsel for the company for years and got along well with the CEO and the Board. Ed felt that he had built a good rapport with Greg. He was certain that getting Greg's input would be key to having his proposal taken seriously. Sure enough, they had a great conversation on the proposed controls. Ed spoke openly about some of the challenges he saw and asked for Greg's perspective. After strategizing over various approaches, Greg told Ed he would absolutely support the direction they had discussed. Ed felt one step closer to making important changes.

Days later, the CEO was in Ed's office, waving a report Ed had prepared for the Board—at the CEO's request. His boss seemed angry. He questioned Ed's motives in writing the report. Based on the words coming out of his boss's mouth, it sounded like Greg had shared some of their conversation—and not necessarily in a supportive way. Ed had trusted Greg with his biggest worries and it sounded like the conversation had been used against him. While he didn't know why, Ed couldn't help but wonder if he had mistakenly been too frank in expressing concerns to his new colleague.

NAVIGATING THIS MINEFIELD: MISPLACED TRUST

Trust is important. It seems virtuous. It is also practical. Trust makes collaboration possible and creates better outcomes. Some level of relational transparency is required in order to have trust. Still, trusting others and being vulnerable is sometimes a bad idea. If you've been burned before, you know this is true. So, what do you do if you aren't sure you can trust a colleague? It's probably best not to test trust with a significant issue. It is part of your human DNA

IT'S NOT ALL SMOOTH SAILING

to have some faith in people, particularly when they seem similar to you. At the same time, experience suggests that people (yes, pretty much all of us) are relatively bad judges of who is and who is not trustworthy. Humans have biases, preconceived notions, and misplaced confidence in others' opinions. All of these things can lead anyone to make a poor judgment call.

How do you know when sufficient trust has been built? It may feel like the only way to test the trust you have in someone is to take a risk and see what happens. There are a few things to consider that could improve your chances of being right.

- Think about your track record of trust. What has it been like?

- If you tend to trust too easily or trust the wrong people, what clues are you missing that you see only in hindsight?

- Which element of trust—dependability, credibility, care, respect, or intention—is the biggest challenge for you when assessing others' trustworthiness?

On the flip side, perhaps you are dealing with a colleague who seems suspicious of you. You wonder what you have done to reduce their trust. Sometimes people project their own insecurities or untrustworthiness onto others. If you are being treated with suspicion, and you are certain you've done nothing to invite such scrutiny, lack of trust may be more about the other person's fidelity or questionable motives.

Adopt enough wariness for self-preservation. At the same time, embrace curiosity and compassion. Where is the bright line between wariness and openness? It will differ from one person to another. Though there is no set formula, sharing less important information selectively at first is one way to confirm trust. Listening to several points of view can also be helpful. And don't discount your intuition. If something just doesn't feel right, listen to your gut and see what more you can learn before you act. Finding the right balance between open and wary will help you navigate difficulties and establish or reestablish more trusting relationships.

CHECK YOUR GPS

Doing the right thing doesn't insulate you from experiencing betrayal or negative consequences. Even when you practice the positive behaviors outlined in this book, there are no guarantees. Minefields and pitfalls may occur at some point in any career. The tools provided here can help you manage over and around the issues that arise. Awareness better prepares you to navigate undesirable realities. In addition, build relationships with other successful leaders. This allows you to draw on their wisdom when you hit a rough patch. While some might view seeking input and suggestions from others as a sign of weakness, collaboration makes everyone stronger. It brings new ideas and perspectives to light. It also makes the leadership journey less lonely.

IT'S NOT ALL SMOOTH SAILING

A SPECIAL NOTE

In spite of everything you have done, you may find yourself at a crossroads. You may decide an organization or the people in the organization are not a good fit with your values. The path they are on is not headed to a destination that interests you. As you consider taking a different route, get clear on whether you are running *to* or running *from*. Taking a new role to escape from a bad situation is the best definition of running *from*. When running from a bad situation, it is important to pause and take a step back. Consider what's going on within you first. It may be helpful to work through the issues with a friend, or better yet, a therapist or coach. Otherwise, it's likely you will take aspects of the situation into your next job. When you are ready to move on, look for opportunities you can be excited about and run toward those instead.

Sometimes you need to leave. The reasons may be simple or complex. You may be crystal clear about resigning or have doubts. Don't simply focus on escape. Be thoughtful in considering what is next for you. "Next" may be a great offer you just received. It could be a break to reconnect with your sanity and recover before your next adventure. It might be a different role in the same organization. Where do you want to go? How can you take steps now to move in that direction? Sometimes you have to leap into the void with limited information about what is out there. Still, having applied the GPS tools with courage and clarity, you can negotiate a soft landing with your respect intact, ready to take on the next challenge.

TRAVEL JOURNAL

As you think about your leadership journey, take a few minutes to consider:

- What minefields and pitfalls have you encountered in the workplace?

- How have you maneuvered around or through these issues? What's been the result?

- Thinking about past challenges, what themes or trends can you identify in how you have addressed each of those problems?

- How can the material in *Courageous Clarity* enhance your ability to avoid or diffuse similar situations?

- Knowing what you know now, what will you do differently in the coming weeks?

Final Thoughts

*"There will come a time when you believe
everything is finished. That will be the beginning."*

— LOUIS L'AMOUR

Every leadership journey is different, and yet there are similarities that allow us to help one another along the way. Courage can be contagious; we find inspiration and encouragement in sharing our stories and challenges. I hope you will continue to benefit from these tools, and to find ways to coach others in their use. Most leaders learn and practice on a journey without end. Often you will encounter other travelers with more time on the path who offer a hand, a word of advice, or a listening ear. The excitement, joy, and challenge are in the journey. Those you meet along the way might support your work, frustrate you, or merely watch as you pass through. When you look closely, there is always opportunity for new discovery and continuous improvement.

As you have followed the GPS methodology, you have learned new concepts or perhaps been reminded of things you've heard before. Maybe you have recognized ideas from your own experiences. While your final destination on the path of successful leadership is not guaranteed, the ultimate direction toward success occurs when these practices are part of your leadership journey:

- Curiosity
- Humility
- Trust
- Transparency
- Flexibility
- Muting yourself
- Feedforward

- Thoughtful responses, rather than reactions
- Conflict management
- Presence and focus as a leader
- Power of noticing
- Communication and influence

These skills—the soft or human skills—sometimes demand relearning. In some cases, significant unlearning is required. This is especially true for successful leaders. What has worked in the past has served you well. Yet to continue to grow may require letting go of past practices and embracing openness to new experiences. You must think differently. Allow yourself to evolve and change. You might sometimes feel you are wandering in the dark. Headwinds will occasionally slow your progress. Detours may avert your trajectory. Dust yourself off and don't give up! Courageous clarity works. I've watched leaders literally transform their careers by practicing these techniques. Yes, it takes a certain level of daring and commitment, but the results can set you on a path to greater opportunity.

FINAL THOUGHTS

NEXT STEPS

The tools you have discovered in these pages will support your continued leadership journey. Here are a few ideas for additional steps you can take.

- Find someone who understands these concepts and will help you tackle each issue with focus. You might share GPS with a friend and support one another in being accountable to the goals you set.

- Maintain a list of curious questions in plain view and check in with yourself daily. What are the key learnings you want to remember? Ask yourself at the end of each day how these discoveries showed up in your leadership.

- When you start to feel defensive, choose to be curious instead.

- When your vision begins to narrow with frustration, pause and ask how you might be redirected to the big picture again.

- Strive to understand emotions and how they affect you and those around you. When you're able to leverage that insight, you can better relate to others' perspectives and intentions.

- Accelerate your progress by engaging a leadership coach. The best athletes use coaches to stretch and continuously improve their capabilities. Business leaders can similarly benefit from the growth that occurs when working with an experienced coach.[1]

TRAVEL JOURNAL

As you prepare to close the cover on this book, look back over any notes you made as you read through each chapter. Perhaps packing list items really resonated. Maybe certain sign posts were most useful to you, or you paused at the caution symbols to reassess because things weren't going as expected. Just as you might check a favorite travel guide when planning your next trip, revisit these concepts from time to time.

- Curiosity, humility, and reflection are leadership strengths. Curiosity is discovery.
- Seek fresh perspectives by asking questions and listening to what others say.
- Trust is the foundation on which great leadership journeys are built.
- Strive to be thoughtful in your responses, not reactionary.
- Stay flexible to observe, anticipate, and bypass issues.
- Manage conflict constructively to help you overcome obstacles.

Even when you do everything right, there will sometimes be cloudy days. How you apply the lessons you have learned can help you stay on track, increase your influence, and lead to better results—for you, your team, and your organization.

FINAL THOUGHTS

For a continued reflection on your leadership journey, take a few minutes and consider:

- Thinking about the jobs you have had over the course of your career, what trends do you see in the roles you have played?
- How have you grown in your work with others over time?
- Which of the GPS concepts can you share with team members to help them develop as leaders?
- With these points in mind, how can you take your career where you want to go?
- What specific steps will you take next to continue to improve as a leader?

Write down your answers as a commitment to yourself to follow through. Then put a reminder in your calendar to formally revisit the related material in *Courageous Clarity*, maybe six months out. What progress have you made? Where will you focus next?

Best of luck with your ongoing leadership journey!

Endnotes

CHAPTER 1

1. Leaders who exhibit curiosity are generally perceived to be more effective. Those leaders enjoy greater engagement and stronger performance from team members. Natalia Karelaia writes of the credibility that comes from asking questions in the *INSEAD Knowledge* article "When in Doubt, Leaders Should Ask Questions." https://knowledge.insead.edu/leadership-organisations/when-in-doubt-leaders-should-ask-questions-13501

2. The importance of self-awareness is explored in more detail in many sources. In a survey of corporate leaders by the Stanford Graduate School of Business Advisory Council, self-awareness was identified as the most important competency for executives to develop (Toegel, G. and Barsoux, J-L. (2012, March). "How to Become a Better Leader." *MIT Sloan Management Review*. https://sloanreview.mit.edu/article/how-to-become-a-better-leader/). Further, psychologist Tasha Eurich notes that 95% of people think that they're self-aware, but only 10–15% actually are. https://www.youtube.com/watch?v=tGdsOXZpyWE. If you want to find ways to work with a boss or colleague who is challenged in this area, Tomas Chamorro-Premuzic offers techniques in his *Harvard Business Review* article "How to Work for a Boss Who Lacks Self-Awareness." https://hbr.org/2018/04/how-to-work-for-a-boss-who-lacks-self-awareness

3. For more information about optimism bias, there is a wealth of data available on both the psychological and neurological bases for human

positivity. Neuroscientist Tali Sharot has authored an insightful book, *The Optimism Bias: A Tour of the Irrationally Positive Brain*. She outlines the benefits and dangers of this uniquely human bias in a TED Talk as well. https://www.ted.com/talks/tali_sharot_the_optimism_bias

4. The brilliant concept of the "idiot test" comes from organizational psychologist and author Roger Schwartz. https://www.schwarzassociates.com/are-your-questions-counterproductive-take-the-you-idiot-test/

CHAPTER 2

1. Confirmation bias can prevent leaders from considering different perspectives. The *APA Dictionary of Psychology* defines confirmation bias as "the tendency to gather evidence that confirms preexisting expectations, typically by emphasizing or pursuing supporting evidence while dismissing or failing to seek contradictory evidence." In other words, people tend to believe what they want to believe and dismiss valid data that challenges those beliefs. Behavioral economists have long studied cognitive biases and the impact they have on decision-making and willingness to hear new information. Some of the more accessible research is reflected in Daniel Kahneman's *Thinking Fast and Slow* and the 2021 edition of *Nudge* by Richard H. Thaler and Cass R. Sunstein.

2. The steps taken by Amara—and thousands of other leaders—to gain insight and improve performance are based on stakeholder-centered coaching, an approach developed by Marshall Goldsmith and refined in collaboration with Frank Wagner and Chris Coffey (https://www.stakeholdercenteredcoaching.com/). The Sarkaria Group, and a number of other excellent leadership coaches worldwide, offer the stakeholder-centered approach for coaching that gets measurable results.

3. For more on feedforward, check out the many resources that Marshall Goldsmith makes available on his website http://www.marshallgoldsmithfeedforward.com/html/FeedForward-Tool.htm.

ENDNOTES

CHAPTER 3

1. Google's internal research on high-performing teams and trust was conducted as part of Project Oxygen where Google's People Analytics team studied the behaviors that make great managers. They then went on to analyze 180 teams to determine what differentiated the teams that were truly successful at Google. You can learn more here: https://rework.withgoogle.com/guides/understanding-team-effectiveness/steps/introduction/

2. Researchers continue to identify trust as a key element for stronger performance. See https://knowledge.wharton.upenn.edu/article/covid-19-teaches-us-importance-trust-work/ for additional information.

3. Though many leaders prefer to avoid conflict, Robert Sutton recognizes that disagreement in a trusting environment can benefit the team, their decisions, and their organization. For more insights to build positive communication skills, check out his book, *Weird Ideas that Work*, and this interview with him: https://www.gsb.stanford.edu/insights/be-better-work-how-communicate-better-coworkers-employees.

4. Empathy is often confused with sympathy, but empathy is not about feeling sorry for others. Empathy includes a wide range of actions such as paying attention to others' emotions, imagining how they might feel, asking questions and listening to understand, and seeing things from their perspective whether or not you agree or have had similar experiences. Researcher, professor, and author Brené Brown talks about the importance of compassion, courage, and connection in cultivating empathy. She has spoken and published numerous works on the subject. One of her books, *Dare to Lead*, draws a clear link for those seeking to be stronger leaders between trust and empathy.

5. When thinking about the bank of trust and its impact on performance, note how deposits and withdrawals in the bank closely correlate with the components of trust. The bank of trust concept is adapted from Stephen R. Covey's *The 7 Habits of Highly Effective People*, which explores emotional bank accounts in greater depth.

COURAGEOUS CLARITY

CHAPTER 4

1. Organizational Behavior Professor Avraham N. Kluger has researched and written extensively on listening as it relates to leadership. His website includes a number of excellent resources on this subject. https://www.avi-kluger.com/

2. For more ideas on ways to grow as a leader, explore Margaret Heffernan's book *Beyond Measure: The Big Impact of Small Changes*. The recommended exercise is adapted from that work. It is a jewel of a book with many suggestions for leaders interested in becoming their best.

3. For more on the subject of hot buttons, awareness, and how to create lasting behavioral change, check out Marshall Goldsmith's bestseller, *Triggers: Creating Behavior That Lasts—Becoming the Person You Want to Be*.

CHAPTER 5

1. For those interested in learning more about honing focus and powers of observation, the Judgment Index includes measures of your ability as a leader to notice, problem solve, and make decisions. It assesses both strength and balance and can be useful for leaders who want to increase their effectiveness and realize their full potential.

2. If meditation, contemplation, or the benefits of training your mind in positive ways are topics you would like to learn more about, Daniel Goleman's extensive work on emotional intelligence and Shirzad Chamine's study of positive intelligence are two sources you might want to explore further. At a basic level, the questions we ask ourselves influence our thinking. For example, what's wrong with work right now? That shifts people to thinking negatively, which is typically an easy transition. A different perspective emerges from asking, what do I enjoy/appreciate about my work currently? Think about it. Begin focusing on more positive outcomes and you are likely to see more of them arise in your day-to-day work.

ENDNOTES

3. The list of management qualities represents a partial collection of top leadership characteristics from Indeed's research. Indeed is not simply a website for connecting talented people with job openings; the company uses its analytical capabilities to identify trends and other useful information. More on Indeed's research on leadership qualities can be found here: https://www.indeed.com/hire/c/info/leadership-qualities-list.

4. For more on the pitfalls of internal competition, see the work of William P. Barnett of the Stanford Graduate School of Business. Known for his "Red Queen" work on competition between organizations, Barnett also provides insights for those wanting to foster more collaborative teams. https://www.gsb.stanford.edu/insights/rethink-competition-workforce

5. In the book *The Four-Fold Way*, Angeles Arrien identified ancient wisdom that is useful in organizational settings. The process of learning and teaching, which Arrien calls "the way of the teacher," highlights wisdom, trust, and detachment, including the concept of being open to, but not attached to, outcomes. Leaders who bring this skill to their interactions with team members and colleagues can improve their performance and that of others.

CHAPTER 6

1. For more on listening with empathy, William Ury's conversation with Bob Chapman on "Real Advice for the Real World" (http://www.trulyhumanleadership.com/?p=2936) has useful insights on how to engage more collaboratively with others.

2. There is a wealth of information available on the Thomas-Kilmann Conflict Mode Instrument that a simple internet search will reveal. A nice summary of the history and design, as well as benefits and risks, of each style can be found here: https://careerassessmentsite.com/tests/thomas-kilmann-tki-tests/about-the-thomas-kilmann-conflict-mode-instrument-tki/.

COURAGEOUS CLARITY

3. For more on the Japanese concept of *nemawashi*, Nigel Thurlow, Chief of Agile at Toyota Connected, created a simple framework for building consensus across organizations based on this practice. You can view it at: https://www.slideshare.net/NigelThurlow/nemawashi-44012407

CHAPTER 7

1. In 1959, John French and Bertram Raven identified sources of power in organizations. Their seminal work continues to be relevant today to anyone thinking about power and politics in their workplace. It is the basis for the descriptions provided here. If you would like to consult the original source to learn more, their book chapter "The Bases of Social Power" is a good place to start. http://www.communicationcache.com/uploads/1/0/8/8/10887248/the_bases_of_social_power_-_chapter_20_-_1959.pdf

2. As you are assessing the power structure and currencies of exchange in your organization, you might review Allan Cohen and David Bradford's book *Influence Without Authority*. Regardless of position (and level of power), leaders can benefit from a closer look at the currencies that are relevant in their organization's culture. Developing your understanding in this area can help you identify the give and take necessary to accomplish your goals.

3. If the idea of Givers and Takers in the workplace intrigues you, you might enjoy reading Adam Grant's book *Give and Take*. He shares more about the interactions and impact of each type in this TED Talk: https://www.ted.com/talks/adam_grant_are_you_a_giver_or_a_taker

4. For more on the study about skills needed for success and the potential implications for your career, Jack Zenger's article on results versus relationships includes additional insight into his work with Joseph Folkman on this topic. https://medium.com/thrive-global/results-or-relationships-which-do-you-value-more-d9c05f2cbccf

ENDNOTES

5. The RACI model is sometimes also referred to as a responsibility matrix because it can serve as a way to better define roles and responsibilities in cross-functional work. If you would like to learn more, RACItraining.com is a helpful resource.

FINAL THOUGHTS

1. If you're interested in exploring the services of a professional coach, some of the best leadership coaches in business today are members of the Association of Corporate Executive Coaches (https://acec-association.org/directory/). You may also reach the author at phyllis@sarkariagroup.com.

Acknowledgments

This book would not have reached completion without the inspiration and encouragement from a wide community of colleagues, friends, family, and thought leaders. At the risk of leaving out many who urged me to take the steps necessary to bring these ideas to print, I would like to express specific thanks and recognition.

This work began because of the clients and colleagues who shared their stories and encouraged me to capture in book format the tools and exercises that we have covered together. Stanley J. Ward served as a vital accountability partner. In the early stages, he provided support, guidance, and just the right amount of pressure to be accountable—all hallmarks of the great coach he is. Without Stan, this book would likely still be a nice idea that I talk about from time to time.

Many thanks are owed to the team that brought the book to life in its final form. Karla Olson is a publishing strategist extraordinaire. She has been an incredible Sherpa for my maiden adventure as an author, assembling a first-rate team: Elaine Cummings is a truly supportive and helpful editor; Laurie Gibson assisted in further refining the manuscript so that it sings; and the creative team at The Book Designers, Alan and Ian, added their talents to produce a professional and accessible final product.

Invaluable observations, input, and ideas from Reba Rose, John Garland, Tracy Cooney, Judy Issokson, Loretta Tolliver, Steve Conrad, Scott Thor, Devyani Bedekar, Chris Huckabee, Desiree Therianos, John Novak, Pepper de Callier, Barrie Hinton, Jack Farnan, and Julie Woolf helped me refine and organize my thinking to create clearer content. In addition, the advice and connections received from Tom Gehring and Maya Hu-Chan were instrumental in moving this forward to completion.

I would be remiss if I did not acknowledge inspiration for the direction I have taken with my coaching from an understanding of mindfulness, dialogue, collaboration, and change that forms the core curriculum of Claremont Lincoln University. Additionally, my work as a coach is strongly influenced by the Berkeley Executive Coaching Institute (BECI). The faculty and staff of BECI—and my BECI colleagues—are doing work that is much needed in organizations today. Thanks to those who challenged, supported, and pushed me to continue to grow, and to get my ideas down on paper. My valued colleagues at the Association of Corporate Executive Coaches have also shared their experiences with writing and publishing, selflessly made introductions, and helped me find my way on this leg of my leadership journey.

Finally, my family. My parents, Tommie and Sylvia Huckabee, have been examples of leadership, love, and faith. Throughout

ACKNOWLEDGMENTS

my life, they have supported my career ambitions and encouraged me to follow my dreams. My brothers, Tim and Chris Huckabee, taught me how to stand up for myself and to subtly influence and mediate disputes before I really understood what that meant. Those early years formed a strong foundation from which my leadership skills have grown. Most of all, my patient, supportive, and loving husband, David Sarkaria, has long been an example to me of true success. His ability to build trust, influence individuals at all levels, and deliver amazing results is truly inspiring. His quiet confidence has buoyed me through various storms. I am blessed to have him as a partner on the journey of life.

Index

A
accountability partners, 5
ambiguity, 106
anger, 90. *See also* triggers
Arrien, Angeles, 106
asking vs. telling, balance between, 25–26, 27, 32

B
Barnett, William P., 105
blind spots, 21, 28
Buffett, Warren, 43–44
Burnison, Gary, 37

C
care, 60–61, 65, 66
Catherine of Siena, 35–36
certainty, desire for, 87–88
clarity
    leadership and, 1
    transparency and, 79–80
    value of, 80–81, 106–7
coaching, 6, 159
collaboration
    competition vs., 105
    conflict and, 126

detachment and, 106
encouraging, 107–8
value of, 93–94, 131
communication
business case for, 112–15
improving, 121–22
influence and, 115–22
role clarity and, 148–51
turf wars and, 151
competition, internal, 105
confidence, 30–31
confirmation bias, 40, 88
conflict
approaches for responding to, 124–26
business case for, 112–15
fear of, 123–24
handling, 126–30
Thomas-Kilmann Conflict Mode Instrument, 124–26
courage
contagiousness of, 157
importance of, 108
leadership and, 1
Covey, Stephen R., 55, 82, 128
credibility, 60, 65, 66
cultural differences, 6–8
curiosity
benefits of, 2, 16, 19–20, 34–35
business case for, 17–20
encouraging, 107
importance of, 31
power of, 35

D

Dalai Lama, 84
dependability, 60, 65, 66

INDEX

discovery
    balancing expertise and, 25
    practicing, 33–34
    spirit of, 16–17
distractions, dealing with, 97–101, 109

E
emotions
    controlling, 73–74, 89
    triggers and, 78, 87–91, 126–27
example, setting an, 73, 79–81

F
failure
    frequency of, 2
    handling, 133
    positive mindset around, 105
fear
    of conflict, 123–24
    of other people's opinions (FOPO), 24–25
    of punishment, 137
feedback and feedforward
    distinguishing, 47
    reflecting on, 47–48
    seeking, 22–24, 44–46
    taking notes on, 46–47
    thanks for, 47
    value of, 45, 46
flexibility
    ambiguity vs., 106
    business case for, 94–96
    opportunities for improving, 107–8
    value of, 93–94, 103–6
FOPO (fear of other people's opinions), 24–25
future, focusing on, 46, 47

G
Givers, 146
Glaser, Judith, 48
Goldsmith, Marshall, 46, 83, 88
GPS acronym
    G (Get Ready), 4, 34, 72
    P (Pay Attention), 4, 52–53, 72, 92
    S (Slow Down to Assess and Adjust), 4, 109, 130–31
Grant, Adam, 145–46

H
Hawkins, Mike, 111
hot buttons. *See* triggers
humility, 30, 31, 35–36, 41

I
"idiot test," 32–33
impressions, importance of, 94–96
influence
    dialogue and, 115–22
    exercising, 119–21
    trust and, 115
intention
    listening and, 82–83
    matching actions and, 74
    trust and, 61–62, 65–66
interpersonal dynamics, 145–47
intuition, 98, 154

J
Jefferson, Thomas, 90
jobs, changing, 155
Johnson, Kate, 93

K
Katzenbach, Jon, 46
Kilmann, Ralph H., 124
Kruse, Kevin, 1

L
L'Amour, Louis, 157
leadership
    approaches to, 26, 27, 28
    characteristics of, 101–2
    clarity and, 1
    courage and, 1
    experience of, 1
    feedback and, 44
    indicators of good, 44
    ineffective, 102
    interactive nature of, 111–12
    as journey, 3–5, 16, 133, 157–59
    trust and, 55–56
listening. *See also* perspective-taking
    exercise, 86–87
    intention and, 82–83
    in meetings, 84–85
    process of, 49–51
    value of, 84

M
Malcolm X, 131
Matchers, 146
meditation, 99
meetings
    increasing productivity of, 107–8
    speaking vs. listening in, 50, 84–85
mistakes, as opportunities, 105
Murphy, Kate, 49

N

nemawashi, 130
noticing, power of, 96–102

O

observation, 96–102
optimism bias, 28

P

past, letting go of, 43–48, 158
perspective-taking. *See also* listening
    benefits of, 37–38, 41
    business case for, 38–39
    description of, 40–41
    questions for, 42
    requirements for, 40
politics, organizational, 134–42
power
    dynamics, 145–47
    position, 138, 139
    referent, 138
    sources of, 137–38
presence
    business case for, 74–78
    components of, 74, 78, 82
    value of, 78–79, 91–92

Q

questions
    importance of asking, 17, 19
    rhetorical, 32–33
    types of, 32

INDEX

R
RACI acronym, 149–51
relationships, nurturing, 143–45, 146
resigning, 155
respect, 61, 65, 66, 129
results, focusing on, 143–45, 146
role clarity, 148–51
running to vs. running from, 155

S
Sagan, Carl, 107
Sandberg, Sheryl, 73
self-awareness
    benefits of, 35
    blind spots and, 21, 28
    cultivating, 21–25, 35
    curiosity and, 16
    humility and, 36
    importance of, 20, 35
    lack of, 21, 26, 39
Sharma, Robin, 15
silence
    intentional, 83
    power of, 48
silos, dangers of, 129
social reciprocity, 69
start-stop-continue exercises, 28–29
stepping back, value of, 38
STOP acronym, 91
survival game, 57–58
Sutton, Robert, 58

T
Takers, 145, 146
"tell-sell-yell" behavior, 48, 117–18
Thomas, Kenneth W., 124
360-degree feedback assessment, 22–24
TKI (Thomas-Kilmann Conflict Mode Instrument), 124–26
transparency, 67–71, 72, 79–80
travel journal, 12–13, 36, 53, 72, 92, 109–10, 131–32, 156, 160–61
triggers, 78, 87–91, 126–27
trust
   assuming, 151–52
   bank of, 63–64
   building, 59, 63, 68, 70
   business case for, 56
   components of, 59–67, 71–72, 153
   importance of, 55–56, 57, 58–59, 71, 152
   influence and, 115
   leadership and, 55–56
   low, 57, 58, 64–67, 153–54
   misplaced, 152–54
   transparency and, 67–71, 72
turf wars, 147–51

U
unlearning, importance of, 158
Ury, William, 115

V
vulnerability, 108

W
WAIT acronym, 51, 115
Ward, Stanley J., 133

About the Author

With more than 30 years of leadership experience, Phyllis H. Sarkaria is a Master Corporate Executive Coach (MCEC) who has worked with companies ranging from start-up and growth phases of the corporate life cycle to those with established, 100+ year old histories. She balances a willingness to push executives to be the best leaders they can be while demonstrating care and respect for their professional fulfillment and success. Phyllis works with leadership teams and individual leaders facing a range of business challenges to identify issues, align people and processes, and move forward with improved results. She holds a BBA, Finance and an MBA from Texas Tech University and an MA, Ethical Leadership from Claremont Lincoln University. She is a published scholar on authentic leadership and has served on several non-profit boards in San Diego and San Francisco, California.

In her spare time, Phyllis and her husband, David, relish active travel and discovering new food and wines. They live in northern San Diego County and enjoy time with three adult children, five grandchildren, and two rascally Airedale Terriers.

Phyllis can be reached at phyllis@sarkariagroup.com.

www.ingramcontent.com/pod-product-compliance
Lightning Source LLC
Chambersburg PA
CBHW050334010526
44119CB00004B/144